FRIENDSHIP
EVANGELISM
IN
YOUTH MINISTRY

by Larry Keefauver

Loveland, Colorado

Dedicated to the ones through whom
I first met the Lord, my parents,
Jim and Sara Keefauver.

Friends & Faith

Edited by Cindy Hansen
Designed by Judy Atwood
Cover Design by RoseAnne Buerge

Library of Congress Cataloging-in-Publication Data

Keefauver, Larry.
  Friends and faith.

  Bibliography: p.
  1. Evangelistic work.   2. Youth—Religious life.   3. Friendship—
religious aspects—Christianity.
I. Title.
BV3793.K35   1986   248'.5   86-7577
ISBN 0-931529-10-7

Printed in the United States of America

Contents

73816

Epilogue   142

Notes   148

Resources   151

Introduction

I carefully planned my first parents' meeting in a church where I was a new pastor. More than 100 families with senior high youth were listed as "active" on the church rolls. By a reasonable estimate, I arranged for a catered meal for around 200 teenagers and parents. I feel that youth ministry is a responsibility of the whole church family, so I invited church staff, lay leaders, teachers, youth workers, as well as teenagers. Reaching out and ministering to young people needs a conscious effort of everyone if we are to be effective.

Excitement built as we decorated the fellowship hall for the dinner. The hour of the dinner finally arrived. Youth began to stream in for the event. Yet, as five, 10, 15 minutes passed, I grew increasingly apprehensive. Parents weren't coming. Church leaders and teachers were absent. Even the church staff was poorly represented. As it happened, only 25 adults came! After dinner, the 25 adults and I sat in a circle and discussed the big question: "Where are all of the adults—the parents, the church leaders, the teachers? Reaching youth for Christ requires all of us. Everyone is needed for youth ministry to be effective—so where is everybody?" Hesitantly one parent volunteered an answer, "In this church, most people think that we hired *you* to do the job."

So that was the expectation! Ministering with youth and their families wouldn't happen until I did it. Not everyone in the church believes that evangelism and ministry are for everyone to do. Some churches get into the mind-set that these tasks are for hire. From that first parents' meeting to now, I have encouraged congregations to involve everyone in youth ministry. No one person should be expected to do the witnessing and discipling that is the work of all of us in the body of Christ.

Reaching out to youth with the Good News of Jesus Christ is the task of the whole church; it is rooted in relationships. Pastors, teachers, church staff, church leaders, parents, adults and peers all develop friendships which model the biblical understanding of God's love, "... there is a friend who sticks closer than a brother" (Proverbs 18:24) and "A friend loves at all times" (Proverbs 17:17). Jesus built on this concept of friendship. He taught his disciples that "Greater love has no man than this, that a man lay down his life for his friends" and "... I have called you friends" (John 15:13-15).

Evangelizing youth is a ministry of friendship in the most profound biblical sense. The befriending process starts in the cradle and proceeds through adolescence. From an early age, the relationships that both adults and other children share with a young person dramatically influence his or her decision to follow Christ. Each relationship lays either a stepping-stone along a path of Christian commitment or digs a pothole distracting a young person from Christ.

If an unchurched teenager's parents have little or no interest in Christianity, then a young person's only opportunity for a Christian relationship may lie with peers. At this point, friends leading friends to Christ become the crucible of evangelism.

Conversion from self-centeredness to Christ-centeredness for a young person rarely happens in isolation. Of course, there are instances when a young person may find a Bible, read it and come to faith in Christ; but many spiritual journeys to Christ follow a circuitous route of relational way stations. For example:

- warm, loving care and a hug in a church nursery,
- parents conveying unconditional love and modeling faith in a child's daily life,
- caring teachers who not only tell but also live out the biblical story,
- a pastor's special times with a young person, and
- congregation members who reach out through financial and program support.

After the foundation has been laid, it's often by an invitation from a friend that a young person confesses, "I believe that Jesus Christ is the Son of God; and I give my life to him in faith."

Relationships are one of the instruments of the Holy Spirit to reach youth. There is nothing new or revolutionary in this affirmation. From Adam and Eve through Noah and the patriarchs, God sought to make himself known through relationships. Adam and Eve started with a relationship with God, but broke it and created a state of sin. Throughout the rest of history, humanity began life separated from God. A relationship with God was no longer a given; it had to be wanted, chosen and desired by each person. Throughout biblical history, God acted in the lives of his people to make himself known. Through people God spoke his Word and revealed his way for relating to him and one another. The relationship was described in the Law (Torah). The relationship was embodied in a covenant with Israel. The relationship was tested and weighed through the prophets. Finally, the relationship needed a personal touch.

God's relationship with humanity found a voice, a touch, a look and a person in Jesus. He began life with a relationship with God, the Father. So, he could say to us, "He who has seen me has seen the Father" (John 14:9). Jesus became the way to a lasting relationship with God, ". . . no one comes to the Father, but by me" (John 14:6). Through Jesus' death and Resurrection, the possibility for a personal relationship with God exists for all persons. That personal relationship was witnessed to by early Christians in forming the church. Through his Spirit, Christ lives in and through his followers touching the lives of others. Genuine friendship in Christ embodies an unconditional love (agape) that affirms and accepts people where they are, just the way they are. Nothing can be done to earn Jesus' friendship and love. They are given freely through grace.

The history of Christianity communicates the Good News of God's love in Jesus Christ through people building relationships with others. People loving others; people becoming friends; friends leading friends to Christ.

Jeremy was part of a new youth group we were forming in our church. The group started small—three to five junior and senior high young people meeting on Sunday evenings for a snack supper, some crazy games, as well as serious discussions. The young people set the meeting agendas. I provided the resources and guidance in applying the Gospel to their needs.

Slowly the group started growing. As the three to five youth built trust and began caring for one another, they started bringing friends. The friends came not because we had the largest or best youth program in town. They came because

7

they were invited by a friend—someone they trusted and knew cared for them.

Jeremy had a friend named Brian. The last time Brian had been in church was as a small child. Something had happened with Brian's parents to turn them off to the church. A deep hurt became a barrier for them. Brian developed into a sharp, intelligent adolescent. He had experienced God's love in his parents indirectly. They would mention that they were Christians and at times, teach him Christian values. But, he was curious. What was Christianity all about, anyway?

Jeremy and Brian were high school friends. They had many common interests including music and scholarships. Jeremy invited Brian to youth group. (I later learned that Jeremy invited Brian several times before he accepted.) Brian finally accepted an invitation. No big deal was made over his coming. The 10 youth group members included him in everything. He had a good time. He discovered that Christians could have fun and be honest with each other. The caring and the fun were genuine. Besides, Brian found the discussion on cults that evening especially stimulating. These Christians also could think, he discovered.

The group continued to grow. Friends inviting and bringing friends. One evening was especially meaningful for Brian. The program was on affirmation from Romans 15:1-13. For one activity, the young people sat in a circle. One person was chosen and the group members took turns affirming him. They each shared one thing they appreciated about the member. This process continued until everyone was affirmed by the whole group.

It was a simple and easy activity for this group of Christian friends, yet something special happened that evening to Brian. He not only heard the affirmations, he felt the wonderful love of Christ coming through those friends. Soon after, Brian came forward in worship and accepted Christ. A few months later, Brian brought two of his friends to Christ—his parents.

This book focuses on specific ways to build relationships which will lead others to Christ. Instead of evangelism just happening, it is much more powerful and effective to sensitize, train and equip adults to build relationships with youth. It is much more exciting to equip young people to reach out to their friends for Christ. That is the purpose of this book.

In this book, we will explore practical ways to build a youth group community of faith. With such a group, churched and unchurched youth affiliate with friends on similar spiritual journeys. With friends they can search for deep personal faith in Jesus Christ. Beyond that, we will discover practical models for youth to share their faith and their search for a deeper relationship with Christ and others. That sharing will go beyond their own youth group members to their school and neighborhood friends who do not know Christ.

One underlying motivation for writing this book was my own personal faith journey. I remember the faces, the kindness, the love and caring from many pastors, teachers, youth sponsors, friends and parents in my path toward Christ. This book is in your hands because they befriended me and led me to Christ. They taught me about friendship evangelism. I want to express my gratitude to the Lord for them: the loving community of the faithful at First Christian Church in Fort Lauderdale, Florida; the nurturing friends in InterVarsity Christian Fellowship (IVCF) at the University of Pennsylvania; the zeal for evangelism that was encouraged in me by Paul Little during a beach crusade with IVCF at spring break; the young people in youth groups from Texas and Florida, who gave me joy whenever one of them brought a friend to Christ.

I also would like to affirm my colleagues at Group Publishing for their support and stimulation in this project, especially Lee Sparks, Cindy Hansen and Gary Richardson who so patiently listened to my ideas. Gratitude also goes to my family—Judy, Amy, Peter, Patrick and new daughter, Missy—who endured the long hours of writing.

This book is dedicated to one best friend. It is because of him and for him that I live. His name is Jesus.

—Larry Keefauver

The Deep Hunger for Relationships

*Y*oung people hunger for deep, meaningful relationships with God and others. The need to relate exhibits itself from birth through death—growing from the cries of infancy to a primal yell for attention, identity, caring and love in adolescence.

A normal child bases relationships on play, friendship and fun. Then, enter adolescence. Teenage relationships bring peer shock to many youth. David Elkind, professor of child study at Tufts University, has documented the transitions from childhood to adolescence in his book **All Grown Up and No Place to Go**. He describes the hunger for relationships and the accompanying shocks:

> Children come together mainly in play groups, and friendships are often determined mainly by who lives nearby. Who gets to play or not to play often depends upon who gets there first or who has the toys or the equipment. Among teenagers, however, belonging to a group is determined by such qualities as social status and ethnic background. As a consequence, many children who felt accepted by their peers as children suddenly experience, as young teenagers, the full impact of social prejudice. This is one type of peer shock, the shock of exclusion.
>
> Second, social interaction among teenagers is different

from that among children. When children socialize, their interactions are generally cooperative and centered on a common activity. Among teenagers social intercourse is much more complex and multilayered. Friendships are based on mutual trust and loyalty . . . Because young people are still relatively inexperienced in these complex relationships, however, they often get hurt. They discover that their trust or their loyalty or their generosity was not reciprocated but rather used and exploited. Teenagers therefore experience a second type of peer shock, namely, the shock of betrayal.[1]

In response to peer shock, the Good News of Jesus Christ is that teenagers can experience inclusive and trusting relationships. Inclusion and trust begin with the unconditional love of God experienced through Jesus' life, death and Resurrection. The environment for experiencing God's love is the church—the youth group. Through accepting and trusting relationships with Christian adults and youth, teenagers can be drawn into a lasting relationship with Jesus Christ. Evangelism will happen if youth ministry builds trusting and inclusive relationships.

Search Institute, in a national research project commissioned by 13 denominations and youth organizations, studied the needs of young teenagers. In the research report "Young Adolescents and Their Parents," 8,000 fifth- through ninth-grade youth responded strongly when asked about needing the relationships of others. Forty-eight percent responded that they worried "very much" or "quite a bit" about "how well other kids like me." And, 45 percent were very concerned about "how my friends treat me."[2] The study found that "networks of friendship become essential for support and advice on how to cope."[3]

Search Institute researcher Merton Strommen reported in **Five Cries of Youth** that young people with low self-esteem desire most "relationship with others" and "to learn how to make friends and be a friend."[4]

In George Gallup's surveys of unchurched youth, young people indicated a deep yearning for a relationship with other caring youth and with God. He writes, "Spiritual nourishment is one of the highest goals that young people presently have.

Relevance is no longer the code word in the religious quest of youth. Get used to a new word: spirituality."[5]

In **The Search for America's Faith**, Gallup reflects that a large measure of the early church's success was in its appeal to secular youth.[6] Friendship evangelism is a key for filling the deep hunger of today's youth for deep relationships and spirituality.

Jesus provides the model for drawing people to him by touching their needs. In the book of John, Jesus looks into the depths of a Samaritan woman's life and promises her: "Every one who drinks of this water will thirst again, but whoever drinks of the water that I shall give him will never thirst; the water that I shall give him will become in him a spring of water welling up to eternal life" (John 4:13b-14). Jesus touches upon the woman's profound need for both a relationship with God (John 4:19-26) and with other people (John 4:16-18). The Gospel touches one of the deepest needs of humans—relationships.

Howard Clinebell, professor of pastoral counseling at the School of Theology at Claremont, articulates the basis of the need to relate.

> We human beings do not just have relationships. In the profound sense, we *are* our relationships. Our personalities are formed by the significant relationships of our childhood. We carry these relationships within us throughout our lives. For better or worse we are, as the Bible puts it, "members of each other." The *will-to-relate* is more powerful than the will-to-pleasure (emphasized by Sigmund Freud), the will-to-power (emphasized by Alfred Adler) or the will-to-meaning (emphasized by Viktor Frankl). This is because it is only in meaningful relationships that we can satisfy our human need for pleasure, power, and meaning or, for that matter, satisfy any other psychological needs. The quality of our ongoing support system and the quality of our inner lives enhance or diminish each other reciprocally.[7]

Youth group relationships provide the essential context for two important goals in evangelism. First, reaching the youth already coming to church. Second, reaching out to friends of church youth.

This book will emphasize deliberate, friendship evangelism and invitation to accept Christ through all the support systems in the church such as Sunday school classes, pastor's classes, confirmation, youth groups and worship settings. Evangelism becomes the actions we take in word and deed through Christ-like relationships.

Jimmy was a real terror in the fifth-grade Sunday school class. He had high intelligence coupled with an emotional disturbance that dated back to preschool. Each new Sunday school teacher was briefed by the predecessor about Jimmy, "the problem child." The fifth-grade teacher believed the worst about Jimmy from the first day of class. She came to me for a solution to the problem. I suggested a number of alternative ways to handle Jimmy's behavior with both love and firmness. I told her, "Talk with him after class. If that doesn't work, have your husband come to class with you and work with Jimmy when he misbehaves. Finally, talk with Jimmy's parents and ask them to come to class and either work with him or leave with him if he misbehaves."

"Those solutions won't work," she insisted. Of course, her words were a self-fulfilling prophecy. The next Sunday she used the method she chose. Jimmy was embarrassed in front of his peers, kicked out of class and ordered to sit in the hall. He was told never to return.

Many Sunday school teachers have been through similar situations not knowing what to do with problem students. "Do I focus on the problem person at the expense of the other students?" Or, "Do I focus on the other students at the expense of the problem person?"

Leaders should be aware of "chronic" cases of misbehavior so that a situation such as this can be avoided. For Jimmy, we set up a classroom of two rather than letting him think, "Since I'm rejected in Sunday school, God must feel the same way about me."

Jimmy and I formed a special relationship over the years. Jimmy accepted Jesus one Sunday morning and was baptized. Eventually, our family moved to another state. A few years later I met Jimmy's parents at a meeting and asked about him. "He's doing very well," they commented. "But we're not going to that church any longer. We go to a new church and Jimmy has had a chance to start over. He's gotten some help from a counselor. By the way, he still talks about you."

If you grew up in the church, recall your Sunday school teachers. Compare how much you learned about the Bible with how much you remember how they treated you, related to you. I remember best what was taught by adults who genuinely cared for me. Relationships are the vessels communicating the love of God.

THE NEED FOR FRIENDSHIP EVANGELISM

Evangelize is a verb—not a noun! In the New Testament, we read of proclaiming the Good News as the action of witnesses. The Greek noun from which we get the word "evangelism" simply translates "good news." Sharing the Good News is to evangelize. The one who shares is the evangelist. Action is everywhere.

The power behind evangelizing action in the New Testament is the Gospel. Paul writes, "For I am not ashamed of the gospel: it is the power of God for salvation to the Jew first and also to the Greek" (Romans 1:16).

Evangelism is the process of Christian witnessing. The process begins with planning, learning and organizing. However, the process never replaces the person. The key to friendship evangelism centers on one friend, sharing his or her friend (Christ), with another friend.

I interviewed a husband-and-wife evangelism team in southern California about their work in the local high schools. My inquiry was simple and direct: "What's effective in high school evangelism and what's not?" The couple reflected that clubs and mass evangelistic techniques were rapidly fading in effectiveness. "The most effective way of reaching these kids is by getting to know them," they stated. Both agreed that the steps to successful youth evangelism were hard work, attending youth activities, understanding their needs and school pressures, and investing large amounts of time in one-to-one relationships.

Friendship evangelism begins with people—not process. Friendship evangelism goes beyond conversion to discipleship. Friendship evangelism is more than winning people to Christ. It's growing people in the image of Christ. "As therefore you received Christ Jesus the Lord, so live in him, rooted and built up in him and established in the faith, just as you were taught, abounding in thanksgiving" (Colossians 2:6-7).

Youth ministry in the local church becomes the ideal setting for friendship evangelism. First, youth ministry provides the training ground for Christian young people to live out their faith, grow in spiritual maturity, and learn how to reach out to others. Second, a youth group can provide for young people what no other social group, club or extracurricular activity can provide: positive affirmation with God's unconditional love.

But, let's not be naive. There are cliques, competition and negative vibes in youth groups. Youth groups can be judgmental and unaccepting toward visitors. But, the goal and direction of youth ministry sets a different tone than most peer groups in our culture. Leaders in youth ministry have the important task of modeling accepting and affirming relationships. Their number-one priority should be to build relationships with and among all the youth. The "peer shock" of exclusion that David Elkind defined is never so devastating as when experienced within a youth group that is supposed to be accepting and loving. Societal groupings foster acceptance based on achievement, competition, economic status and popularity. Within the Christian community there is the hope for acceptance on the basis of individual self-worth. People are loved for who they are, not for what they've achieved or how successful are their parents. So a youth group represents a safe environment. A Christian young person can discover security, affirmation, love and acceptance within a youth group at church. The youth group is not a guilt trip but a place for making friends, exploring new ideas, asking questions and growing closer to Christ and his people.

Ideally, a youth group should be the one safe place for Christian young people to bring non-Christian friends for:

● acceptance—not put-downs,

● worth based on God-given dignity—rather than achievement,

● friendship based on caring and giving—rather than taking,

● growth based on seeking—rather than being told what to think,

● unconditional love from God and his people.

Christian youth can reach out in friendship to non-Christians by sharing Christ in words and actions. Christian youth don't have to be Lone Rangers in evangelism. Given a positive youth ministry setting, youth group members support each other to foster their own spiritual growth, to provide a positive place to bring non-Christian youth, and to share their faith with their friends.

The relational model of Philip and Nathanael fits here. In John 1:43-51, Philip discovers faith in Christ and then invites Nathanael to meet Jesus. The key to the story is, "It takes a friend to bring a friend to Jesus."

I read a poignant recollection written by a prisoner after a visit from his father:

> I saw my father today
>   After six years.
>   He stayed for 10 minutes,
>   Not knowing
>   What to say
>   Or how to take
>   The glass between us.
>   He left $50,
>   Asking if it were enough.
>   I told him, 'It's more than I make,
>   In two months' work.'
>   I didn't tell him
>   That it couldn't buy six years
>   Or that it was worth far less,
>   Than six more minutes.[8]

The son needed a gift worth far more than anything he could earn. He needed the time and friendship of his father. So the Christian gives a gift which no person can earn. There is a difference between dropping off the gift and running away and giving the gift and ourselves. Martin Marty in his book **Friendship** comments that "What a friend we have in Jesus" might in fact mean "What a Jesus we have in a friend."[9] Witnessing begins with a person and a relationship. The qualities that we need for witnessing are not specialized skills; they are relational skills. To be a friend means to notice, care and become involved.

Jesus noticed Philip. Jesus sought out Philip. Look closely at the text. "The next day Jesus decided to go to Galilee. And he found Philip ..." (John 1:43). The lost need to be found. The lonely need to be met where they are. Then Jesus invited Philip to "follow me." How did Philip share his discovery of the Christ? "Philip found Nathanael, and said to him, 'We've found him of whom Moses in the law and also the prophets wrote, Jesus of Nazareth, the son of Joseph' " (John 1:45).

Nathanael wondered if anything good came from Nazareth, and Philip just said, "Come and see." Philip didn't argue or get into a debate. He didn't prove how much his life had changed. He didn't demonstrate how much he knew about the scriptures or try to manipulate Nathanael. Philip simply invited Nathanael to see for himself.

That's the kind of invitation young people can give to their friends. Surveys tell us that people come to Christ primarily through an invitation from a friend. Following are similar findings of how people become part of Christian communities:

.01 percent through crusades,
1 percent through church visitation,
4 percent through church programs,
4 percent through the pastor or simply by walking in,
70 to 90 percent through the invitation of a friend.[10]

The conclusion is simple. Friends bring friends to Christ. Even in massive evangelistic campaigns, relationships form the foundation for most conversions. A couple of years ago my youth group members were counselors and active participants in the Billy Graham Crusade in south Florida. The Graham association indicated that the largest numbers of people coming forward in any crusades were young people. At the precrusade youth rallies and crusade meetings, hundreds of youth accepted Christ. Where did all of these youth come from? There's no mysterious formula. Christian youth invited their non-Christian friends to the meetings and led them to Christ after the meetings. After the crusade, the new Christians went with their friends to youth groups to continue their walk with Christ.

The majority of persons come to a personal faith in Christ in their older elementary and teenage years. When asked the question of where the church's evangelistic effort needs to be focused, one Christian journal astutely answered, "Forty-six percent of the United States population is under age 25. That should give you a clue."[11]

Another evangelism statistic comes to mind. "Eighty-five percent of persons will not become Christians unless they do so before age eighteen."[12] Jesus' commission to his disciples directs our mission (Matthew 28:18-20). Evangelistic action is mandated by Christ. Youth ministry can become an exciting evangelistic setting for bringing youth to a living, personal faith in Jesus Christ. Friendship evangelism is person-to-person with the Good News of Jesus Christ touching the deepest needs of youth.

YOUTH NEEDS

Friendship evangelism begins within the church during those early preschool years. John Westerhoff describes these formative years of faith as a "journey together in faith." A child experiences the faith from the entire community of the church. A child then affiliates with that community. Westerhoff reflects:

> From the start, a child's life includes others outside the immediate family. Thus the gift of faith is directly related to a family's participation in a community's rituals, symbols, and myths. Affiliative faith looks to the community and its tradition as its source for authority. We depend on significant others for the stories that explain our lives and how our people live. Belonging to a community is very important in order to fulfill our need to be wanted and accepted.[13]

Experiencing the faith through the Christian community is an applicable insight for youth ministry. The youth group is often comprised of youth who have grown up in the church and have similar faith experiences. They feel comfortable and accepted by one another and the adult leaders. The youth individualize and personalize their faith by sharing with one another. This happens as the young people search out the meaning of their faith for personal understanding and growth. Through building a close-knit youth fellowship, the context for searching is provided. Youth can ask questions and reach out honestly to fill emotional, intellectual and spiritual needs.

In some circles of youth ministry, evangelism is conceived as answering all questions, removing all doubts, and having youth act like clones of the adult leaders or other youth who "have it all together." Youth ministry that fears searching often sets up youth for future faith crises in their young adult years. By accepting doubts, dealing honestly with questions, affirming the worth and value of each young person, youth ministry in a local church provides the opportunity for what Westerhoff calls searching faith:

> Searching faith, possible for many adolescents, begins during high school years and extends through early adulthood. It is characterized by questioning, critical judgment, and experimentation ... To find a faith of our own, we need to doubt, question, and test what has been handed down to us ... During this period, it is not faith that is lost, but the expressions of faith which belonged to others and which need to become our own if they are to influence our lives.[14]

Friendship evangelism requires the building of positive relationships within the youth group and the searching for a deeper relationship with Christ and others. These relationships grow as they meet the deep needs of youth.

We often stop before we start in evangelism, because we are controlled by negative and pessimistic attitudes. We choose to believe that youth are overwhelmingly negative about the institutional church. That's only a partial truth. According to a Gallup survey, youth are negative about certain issues:

● the church's failure to serve genuinely the Christ we claim to love and obey,

● the inability of the church to communicate the faith to youth with a sound spiritual basis,

● the lack of excitement, warmth and enthusiasm in church worship and fellowship,

● the low personal standards of some clergy.[15]

Gallup's surveys reveal that youth link the church with other American institutions of which they are critical, for example, the military, big business, Congress and labor unions.

Hence, the church is and must be different. Something must distinguish it from the rest of society. While the church cannot shed all of its institutional trappings, it must develop a youth ministry that meets the needs of young people as can no other institution or group within society. The good news is that the Christian faith touches youth as can no other club, school function, extracurricular activity, or athletic team. Deep needs of youth for spirituality, meaningful faith and service, and for a group that accepts and affirms are best met by a Christian youth group. Youth are asking for a faith that means something in daily life. They "resent the failure of the churches to deepen their perception of God and to widen their experience in spiritual pursuits."[16]

Debra's parents went to our church. She didn't. While visiting all the inactive youth in our congregation, I stopped by to talk with Debra. She was neither a cheerleader nor a scholar. Words to describe her came to mind: plain, homely, shy, average, overweight, acne, needing braces. Everything she said and all her non-verbal behavior pointed to a low self-image. Now, where would she find acceptance and love? Where would she be affirmed and not ridiculed? I told her the youth group needed her. She would find a super group of exciting people who liked being together. The youth group really loved Christ and one another. Everyone fit in and participated in activities they chose. Nobody was asked to do something at youth meetings that would embarrass him or her. Debra believed me. Unfortunately, I was wrong!

Oh, I had the right idea about our group. The problem was we hadn't arrived yet. Debra went Sunday evening to youth group. The girls ignored her. One junior high boy teased her about her weight and teeth. That's all it took. The next week Debra stayed home and watched television during the youth meeting.

My mistake was obvious. I hadn't prepared the young people to reach out for Christ. I had assumed that because they had accepted Christ, evangelism would be automatic. Wrong! Their attitudes at school had shaped the youth group: cliques, put-downs, valuing people by what they wore and how they looked. The deep yearnings of youth for spirituality, love and acceptance were not yet being met. I had to take some important steps to help us grow from a selfish youth group to a caring one. Many of the steps that were taken are detailed in this book. They worked. Debra is one of the reasons for this book. Months later, she not only came back to church, but stayed. She found that Christ was the center of her life. She discovered deep, meaningful friendships within the youth group. Her low self-esteem became self-confidence. She lost weight, wore braces and dressed well. She had met someone who made her feel good about herself. That someone, Jesus, made himself known through 40 other Christian youth group members.

Some leaders try to win the "cream of the crop" for Christ and then hope the rest of the youth will follow. This strategy pivots on teenagers' needs for acceptance, the desire to be liked, to be at the top. Yet, most youth are not the popular school athletes, not the popular school leaders, not the brightest and best students. There's nothing wrong with athletes reaching athletes and leaders reaching leaders, but friendship evangelism doesn't stop there. Friendship evangelism encourages and equips youth to reach both their friends and to reach out beyond to make new friends for Christ. Something very special happens in a youth group when a young person who "has everything" befriends one who doesn't. The bond they share is Christ. The deep relationship grows because each one accepts the other unconditionally. The athlete or scholar discovers that the new friend has unique and special gifts that minister to his or her needs. The new friend who isn't the most popular youth discovers that the athletes, scholars and school leaders have deep needs. They hurt. They are lonely. They sometimes feel insecure and inadequate.

Some 200 youth group leaders gathered at a retreat center in central Texas. They were the best leaders, students and mature Christians in their youth groups and districts. The opening exercise called for individual reflection. On a 3×5 card the young people were asked to complete this sentence: "I'm loneliest when . . ." They were asked not to sign the card. The cards were collected and then read later in the session. All of the retreat participants were shocked at the volume and deep cries of loneliness among these "cream-of-the-crop" youth. One wrote, "I'm loneliest when I lay in my bed at night and hear my parents fighting." Another wrote, "I was lonely when I broke up with my boyfriend." Still another, "The night my best friend killed himself, I cried all night."

Everyone realized that we all hurt. We all need each other. We all long for the touch of Christ. As Paul writes, "If one member suffers, all suffer together; if one member is honored, all rejoice together" (1 Corinthians 12:26).

When teenagers discover a place where all people are accepted, not for what they've achieved or what they have, but simply for who they are, they will come. Youth groups will grow when they meet young people's deep needs for spirituality, acceptance and affirmation.

That kind of youth ministry doesn't just happen. Through the entire church's ministry with children and youth, adults must work at building positive relationships with youth. Adults need to be equipped to share Christ in many different ways through each youth activity—Sunday school, choir, worship, youth meetings, church athletic teams, etc.

Every person involved in youth ministry in the church is critical to reaching out for Christ. Adults and youth together become effective witnesses. Once adults form relationships with young people, the adults can begin to share their faith and equip the young people to reach out to their friends. However, adults can take youth evangelism just so far. Donald McGavran, an early author in the church growth movement, identified people movements as central to evangelistic strategy. Friendship evangelism takes seriously the simple reality that youth can lead their friends, entire groups at school and their neighborhood to Christ.

Jan lived down the street from our church. One afternoon after school, she visited our church's youth center. She enjoyed herself and met some new friends from the youth group as well as other friends she already knew from the surrounding neighborhood. In a few weeks, Jan brought her sister to the youth center. They both came to the youth group on the invitation of one of the Christian youth working as a volunteer in the youth center. Next, the two sisters brought their best friends. Within six months, all were active in the youth group and choir. Both sisters accepted Christ. People reaching people, person-to-person.

In "Young Adolescents and Their Parents" (referred to earlier in this chapter), Search Institute identified the most pressing needs of young teenagers:

● having a happy family life,

● getting a good job,
● doing something meaningful with my life,
● doing well in school,
● world peace.

Young people worry most about:
● school performance,
● my looks,
● how well others like me,
● the death of parents,
● how my friends treat me.

Other important needs and issues for young adolescents are being liked by friends, feeling good about myself, hunger and poverty in the United States, losing my best friend and having a relationship with God.[17]

In the following chapters, our task is clear and well-defined. How do we equip adults and youth in the church to reach youth within the church? How do we move beyond ourselves and reach unchurched youth for Christ? How do we develop a relational youth ministry program that meets the deep needs of youth through the power of Christ? How do we develop relationships between adults and youth that verbally and non-verbally communicate the Good News of Jesus Christ? How do we equip youth to reach out to one another through caring relationships? *How can our youth groups grow?*

The desire to build youth group attendance springs from the sincere desire to tell others about the Good News of Jesus Christ. The answer is both simple and complex. Growth in youth ministry takes desire, equipping, much effort, and the deep love of Christ. Friendship evangelism offers basic principles and concrete steps for growth. This book addresses those steps so that your youth group and youth ministry can grow— not for the sake of numbers alone—for the sake of Jesus Christ and his Kingdom. Let's witness and grow together for him!

Chapter Two

Reaching Our Own

*P*arents are faced with the awesome responsibility of sharing the faith with their children. By grace, we are not alone. The church forms an extended family for witnessing to and nurturing children. Reaching the children within our own church becomes a cooperative task. Everyone is needed—pastor, church staff, teachers, youth workers, athletic coaches, parents and church members.

For effective evangelism, every church member must be trained to share the faith through their relationships with the children and youth. Even the most casual relationship offers an occasion for evangelism. In visiting a neighborhood church one Sunday evening, my 7-year-old son listened to the preacher. Undoubtedly, the preacher felt his message was evangelistic. He gestured dramatically and the decibel level of his voice increased to thunderous tones. My son asked in a loud, hoarse whisper, "Why is that man yelling at us, Dad?"

In another church setting, visitors were asked to remain seated during a moment of fellowship and introductions. All the members of the church stood. While towering over us, the members introduced themselves to the visitors. My family and I were quite intimidated. What was overtly evangelism became a non-verbal threat. Subtle, isn't it? Yet, children and teenagers are very sensitive to how church members treat them. Children often interpret the actions and attitudes of

Christian adults to be God's attitudes and actions.

In the mid-1960s, churches were embroiled in civil rights. Some activist black groups forcibly integrated churches. During that period, the members of our youth group attended a special board meeting of church officers. In our youth group meetings, we had studied and discussed Christian attitudes about civil rights. One of the church leaders visited our youth meeting and talked about how the church should welcome people of all ethnic backgrounds. He had affirmed that God's love extended to everyone. Yet, during the board meeting, the same man proposed a motion to militantly deny entrance to any blacks who tried to attend our worship service. The youth at the board meeting were shocked. Some disillusionment arose. A few never came back to the youth group. That one man's inconsistent and negative witness turned some young people away from Christ. Friendship evangelism is everyone's responsibility in the church; our actions and words are taken seriously by young people.

Our task is to raise the awareness of all church members to the witness they make for Christ with children and youth. The church must train and equip adults for evangelism. That training is more than just talking about it from the pulpit (as important as that is). Raising awareness entails more than asking children and youth if they are saved or if they love Jesus. The equipping process begins with parents, then Sunday school teachers and nursery workers. It extends to custodians and youth workers, worship leaders and church officers. Let's look at the different people involved and how they can be sensitized to their evangelistic roles with church youth.

INVOLVING PARENTS

Parents play a key role in effective youth ministry. Without their support and active involvement, much of what is begun at church will be undone in the home.

The first step in developing parental support is through regular contacts between youth workers and the parents. This is done through a variety of means. A weekly or biweekly postcard or newsletter keeps families informed about youth group activities. A youth column in the church newsletter and Sunday morning bulletin also communicates well with parents. Periodic telephone calls to both youth and parents establish personal contacts. Home visitations build positive foundations for relationships and involvement with parents.

So what have these steps to do with evangelism? Remember, the first step in friendship evangelism is to *establish* a relationship. It's important to remember that the parents need cards, phone calls and visits just as the young people do. Parents need to know and trust the adults to whom they send their youth for activities. A young person talking about the youth workers to his or her parents never replaces personal contact between youth workers and parents.

An important dimension in friendship evangelism is that both youth and youth workers may become witnesses to parents not involved in the church. Too often I have observed youth ministry settings that alienate youth and parents. At times the irrational choice is posed to youth—either follow your parents' wishes or the wishes of the youth group. No purpose is served when youth ministry competes with parent-youth relationships. If a young person's parents are non-Christians, then the loving, caring relationship could bring the parents to an understanding of God's love.

Friendship evangelism can become an outreach to the whole family. Parents are encouraged to attend parents' meetings which can be held every three to four months. At these meetings, youth leaders and workers explain the youth ministry program. Calendars and information about upcoming events are distributed. Parent volunteers are recruited to prepare snack suppers, provide transportation, help in fund raising, chaperon events and numerous other tasks. The program and curriculum materials are shown to the parents. The purpose and goals of the church's youth ministry are explained. (Another benefit for parents is the support and understanding they can give to and receive from other parents.)

Let's look at an example of effective friendship evangelism: Both Mark and his parents had attended the church for years but never had become very active. When Mark reached junior high, he started attending both Sunday school and youth meetings. He became excited about his faith. Before long, he was studying and reading everything he could about Christ. He talked seriously about his faith to his parents and demanded to know why they weren't more involved in their faith. This began to irritate Mark's parents. They came to me one evening after a youth meeting and wanted to know why I was turning Mark into a religious fanatic. They felt very threatened by Mark's enthusiasm for Christ.

How could a youth worker handle a situation similar to this one?

1. Ask the parents to listen to Mark. Perhaps they are lukewarm in their faith and need to be enthusiastic like him.

2. Defend Mark's enthusiasm, explaining how important Christ is to him.

3. Begin witnessing to them about Jesus Christ, in whom Mark has entrusted his life.

4. Listen carefully and seek to understand the feelings of Mark's parents.

Any of the above options might work, but the fourth option stands the best chance for establishing a relationship with Mark's parents. If they can see that the youth worker cares just as much for them as for Mark, they might begin to trust the youth worker. With that trust comes the opportunity to involve Mark's parents. They might be invited to the next parents' meeting or support group. The youth worker could offer to discuss the youth ministry program with them. Friendship evangelism would initiate a relationship with both Mark and his parents, striving to win the entire family to Christ.

Our most effective model for a parents' support group was short-term parent studies during youth meetings. While the young people went to youth groups, the parents stayed at church and studied topics that would equip them to be more effective parents. These discussion groups lasted four to six weeks and were held two or three times a year. That way we didn't burn parents out but still provided a setting in which they could hear what other parents were experiencing and how they were coping.

One effective series involved Dr. James Dobson's film series **Focus on the Family**, from Word Films.[1] At other times, we discussed issues or concerns such as dating and rules, discipline, study habits, rock music and peer influence. An exciting resource for parent study and discussion in support groups is "Parent's Page" in Group's JR. HIGH MINISTRY magazine.[2]

In these support groups, committed Christians shared how their faith in Christ strengthened them as parents. This spontaneous sharing brought the non-Christian parents closer and to a deeper seeking of how the Christian faith supported family life. We discussed ways parents could witness to youth. These were the same techniques we taught to teachers and youth workers. The key here was the parent-youth relationship. We explained that youth observe their parents' lifestyle every day. Youth see a positive witness in their parents if there is grace before meals, times of prayer and Bible reading, family discussions and demonstration of their Christian values.

Some specific ways that parents can share their faith with their children are:

● attending worship regularly with youth;

● discussing the sermon with youth after church;

● going together to an intergenerational Sunday school class or church fellowship group;

● praying together at home;

● reading and discussing the Bible together—not the parent reading the Bible to children and asking questions, but a mutual sharing;

● going together to school functions, concerts or movies and afterward discussing the activities (for example, viewing and discussing a movie such as **Places in the Heart** or the classic video **A Man for All Seasons**);

● sharing beliefs during non-conflict times when important issues can be discussed without argument or hard feelings. Often such discussions may be raised by "What if . . ." kinds of questions:

"If your best friend became pregnant, what advice would you give her?"

"If someone you knew at school was thinking about suicide, what would you do?"

"If I, as a parent, saw a friend of yours shoplifting, what do you think I should do?"

"One of our neighbors asked about our youth group and if I thought his daughter would enjoy herself if she came. What should I tell him?"

"What if our government forbade free worship and arrested anyone caught with a Bible. What would you do?"

"How do you think Christ feels about nuclear weapons?"

"Should an unwed mother keep her baby or give her baby up for adoption?"

The list is endless. But, it seems that we as parents never talk about vital issues of faith until there's a crisis or problem. So much witnessing could be done if parents would initiate conversations with their teenagers when the atmosphere is peaceful instead of charged with conflict. Parent support groups meeting throughout the year provide a setting for parents to learn how to talk with their teenagers and share their faith. By sharing with one another, parents discover insights into their own problems and concerns and uncover ways to talk with their teenagers about Christ in real, rather than artificial ways.

CHURCH LAY LEADERS AND STAFF

Lay leaders convey to young people their worth within the body of Christ—and implicitly their worth to Christ—by the decisions they make affecting church youth. If church leaders place a high priority on youth ministry, the young people get the message that who they are and the things they do are very important.

For example, if lay leaders refuse to adequately finance the youth programs, teenagers begin to feel that they're not important. If youth believe that church leaders are inspired by God to lead the church, and the leaders ignore the young people, they will conclude that God feels they are unimportant to the body of Christ. Youth are often unmotivated to go to church or participate in youth activities because they feel that the adults simply don't care. The young people surmise that if God's people don't care about them then God doesn't either.

One youth group I visited was given a small classroom in a back corner of the educational building for all of their activities. Only months before, the church had built a beautiful, costly sanctuary. I asked the young people why they didn't come to Sunday school or youth groups, or why they didn't bring any friends with them to church. Their response was simple: "This church builds everything for adults, not youth. Who wants to come and sit in a small classroom on Sundays when we have to go to school every week? There's no place for us here."

Another church I visited allotted no money for the youth groups. The kids had to raise money for everything they

29

wanted to do through fund-raising projects. After a few years filled with fund raisers, the adults got tired of paying to go to youth events and complained to the board. So, instead of adding funds to the budget to cut back on all the fund raisers, the board simply outlawed fund-raising projects. Needless to say, the youth groups were very discouraged. Amazingly, the board members asked me to find out why the youth didn't want to come to church! The answer was right in front of them.

Youth get excited about church when adults are excited about them. Youth are enthusiastic about bringing their friends to a church that places a high priority on youth ministry. The conclusions for friendship evangelism are obvious. It's impossible to relate to youth in a church where they feel unwanted and unimportant. It's difficult to invite youth to come to a church that doesn't have a "place for the youth." They need their own rooms, their own programs, their own teachers and workers who relate specifically to them. Church leaders investing money, providing facilities and recruiting volunteers to work with youth form a foundation for friendship evangelism to happen.

I once served a church in Texas as an associate minister. My primary responsibilities were in education and youth ministry. I discovered that the youth classes and groups had been shuffled around all over the church building; almost yearly the youth rooms were relocated. When I arrived, they were meeting in the basement. The youth rooms had tile floors, vanilla walls (posters and banners couldn't be hung on walls), metal folding chairs, and dropped ceilings with bright lights. There were no windows. Massive metal gates with imposing bars stood across the stairwells leading to the basement. The youth area looked like a juvenile detention center.

I went to the church administrator and immediately scheduled evening youth meetings in the church parlor. He almost fainted. The church parlor was a large, carpeted room with comfortable furniture, expensive interior decorating and windows. Few youth had ever set foot in the parlor, much less had a meeting there. Still, no other group had scheduled Sunday evening meetings there so the room was available.

The young people loved the room. They carefully moved all the non-functional furniture against the walls and sat on the floor. It was a wonderful setting for high-energy activities.

Soon after we started holding our youth meetings in the church parlor, some church leaders scheduled a special luncheon with me. They expressed concern about the youth needing a place of their own. I shared with them the dreams the youth had for renovating the basement. The youth had plans to install carpet halfway up the walls as well as on the floor. They were raising money for carpeting, comfortable furniture and paint.

The leaders committed themselves to raising over $15,000 to renovate the basement for the youth.

The church leaders were impressed by the number of inactive and unchurched youth who were beginning to come to the meetings. The story's ending is predictable. When the youth saw how committed the church was to them, they became more involved in the church's total ministry and invited their friends to youth activities.

Church staff members are critical in effective friendship evangelism. The choir director needs to minister to youth as well as adults through his or her selection of music. Or, the choir director can form a separate youth choir which sings music that meets their needs. A church secretary should be willing to send out mailings to the youth and to their unchurched friends. A custodian needs to work with youth in maintaining their church facilities rather than criticizing youth for "messing up things." The basic message that church staff and lay leaders will communicate is that youth are important to Christ.

To build a foundation for friendship evangelism, church leaders need to:

● provide a place or facility where youth can meet and feel good about bringing their friends;

● recruit and train youth teachers and youth workers;

● provide adequate funding for youth programs and materials;

● be willing to commit church staff time to youth programming;

● publicize youth activities;

● involve youth in the church's total ministry;

● utilize youth in the church's visitation program (when new families with children visit the church, have active Christian youth equipped in friendship evangelism visit those families);

● make youth highly visible in the church's worship service through singing in choirs, reading scripture, leading prayer, and working as ushers and greeters.

FRIENDSHIP EVANGELISM BEGINS IN EARLY CHILDHOOD

Evangelism begins at the earliest levels of learning in the church. Trained, caring adults convey the faith through their relationships with children.

The nursery experience builds an evangelistic foundation. Young parents will bring children to the church nursery only if it's well-staffed and adequately equipped with the right furnishings, toys, and is safe. Wait a minute. This book is about friendship evangelism among youth. Why are we talking about the nursery? First, because the nursery is a starting point for a young person to build an understanding of God. Second, it is a place where many youth serve the church. The nursery becomes a place for young people to share the faith with small children, thus reinforcing what they know of God and his love.

The nursery and preschool are foundational for building a child's understanding of God. Instead of hiring just anyone who's willing to work on a Sunday morning, the church needs to utilize trained, highly skilled and very sensitive Christian adults. Often church members think, "Let's find someone outside the church to hire for the nursery." However, there may be people within the Christian community who are gifted in the ministry to small children. Jesus placed ministry to children and the cultivation of their faith as one of his highest priorities.

Whoever receives one such child in my name receives me; but whoever causes one of these little ones who believe in me to sin, it would be better for him to have a great millstone fastened round his neck and to be drowned in the depth of the sea.

See that you do not despise one of these little ones; for I tell you that in heaven their angels always behold the face of my Father who is in heaven (Matthew 18:5-6, 10).

The following factors are important for an effective nursery and preschool setting:

1. Hire consistent persons who have a solid, personal faith in Christ and regard working with small children as a ministry.

2. Maintain a ratio of one adult to five children. Some of the workers can be junior or senior high youth.

3. Plan regular training meetings for nursery workers and preschool teachers. Emphasize the following points during the training:

● hug and hold the children, lead them by the hand, play games that involve safe and fun touch;

● equip workers and teachers with children's Bible story books available at Christian bookstores;

● provide children's filmstrips and videotapes with Bible stories;

● plan occasions for parents, preschool teachers and workers to discuss the program and their respective expectations;

● set up written guidelines for parents, teachers and workers to follow regarding both the teaching and care of children;

● teach both parents and youth to assist in caring for preschoolers.

Denominational and interdenominational publishing houses provide an abundance of curricula and training materials for nursery and preschool workers. Your pastor or Christian education director can supply catalogs and resources for training and teaching.

How do the nursery and preschool fit into friendship evangelism beyond being a foundation for faith formation? When teenagers share their faith with nursery and preschool children, the teenagers' faith is then strengthened, reinforced and developed.

Implement this model of friendship evangelism by taking these steps:

1. Be committed to your initial purpose and motives. Some churches use, and even abuse, the services of youth in this area. The church might desperately need help in the preschool or nursery so the young people are drafted to do what adults won't do. The purpose in this evangelism strategy is to hire already committed Christian *adults* to work with the nursery and preschool. These adults should provide excellent care and learning opportunities for the children, yet they also should be willing to supervise and teach the teenage helpers.

2. Plan two or three 90-minute training sessions to orient the youth to the nursery and preschool procedures and introduce them to basic teaching techniques. Keep the training period brief. The temptation is to put the youth through a long training process. However, if the training takes too long, the youth will become disinterested and bored and drop out of the program.

3. Emphasize this experience as a ministry and service for Christ and the church, not a way to skip Sunday school class or the worship service.

4. Set definite time limits on the project. For example, train the young people during two or three Sunday afternoons. Let them observe the class they will be assisting with. Let the teenagers work in the nursery and preschool for a period of one or two months and then have them return to their own class or the worship service. Then at a later time, the young people can serve again for a one- or two-month period.

5. Train the young people to create and present teaching projects. For example: "Tell a story about Jesus or a parable in such a way that a 2-year-old or 3-year-old would understand it. Use whatever props or materials you can find or make to tell the story. To present the parable of the sower (Matthew 13), you could find rocks, weeds, seeds, dirt and other objects to present each type of soil."

Once the youth understand the need for being very concrete and visual with the children, ask them to create object lessons and stories. Work with the youth on how to explain concepts like incarnation, Resurrection, God's love, the cross and sin. As the young people struggle with what these concepts mean to themselves, they grow in faith.

A concrete way to show sin and forgiveness is to gather all of the children in a cluster and wrap yarn around them several times. Ask them to try to walk while they are bound. Say that this is like sin. Use scissors to cut the string. Ask the children to move around. Say that this is like Christ's forgiveness. Talk about how it felt to be tied up and then set free.

Liesl assisted the nursery and preschool workers for a number of years for short periods of time. On her own, she took an intensive teacher-training course in our church. As a high schooler, she kept pace well with the adults in the course. Then she taught a children's class in the summer to give one of the adult teachers a rest. Throughout the summer, she invited other youth to help her. Some of the young people found themselves teaching about biblical concepts they had only recently begun to understand. The amount of spiritual growth they experienced outpaced what they would have received in going to their own class. They learned quickly from Liesl through on-the-spot training. Liesl was evangelizing her peers through this teaching relationship. They were becoming excited about their relationship with Christ through working with the younger children.

This model works with both preschool and elementary children. It works best when older youth are involved. Junior high youth are especially helpful in nursery and preschool classes, summer children programs or vacation church schools. High school youth work well with both preschool and elementary children. Youth also are excellent counselors in after-school programs working with unchurched elementary children. Except in unusual situations, it is best to have young people work in teaching for short periods of time, returning to learning settings with their peers.

EFFECTIVE TEACHERS AND YOUTH WORKERS

We have identified two important concepts for reaching our own. First, reaching our own is the task of the entire church. Second, friendship evangelism begins at the earliest levels of learning. We add to these concepts that evangelism occurs within the teaching relationship.

The teaching relationship takes place within the settings of both the Sunday school classes and the youth groups. Churches make an artificial distinction between teachers and youth workers in the ministry of the church. In fact, teachers and youth workers need the identical skills for reaching youth for Christ. Both need to build positive relationships with youth. Both teach by lifestyle as well as by communicating the content of the Gospel. Teachers and youth workers need to work together to reach youth for Christ. In some churches, teachers and youth workers never meet, never discuss mutual concerns, never pray, plan or train together. Yet, both are working with the same youth for the same purpose—to evangelize and disciple youth in Jesus Christ.

The teacher and youth worker relationship embodies invitation. By invitation, we mean the call of Christ, "Come and follow me." If we dissect the nature of that call, such words come to mind as trust, faith, commitment, obedience, service and love. All of those words are appropriate when describing the relationship a Sunday school teacher and youth worker have with youth. The meaning of Christ's invitation becomes real or "incarnate" as the teacher and youth worker live out their relationships with Christ and young people.

Sit back and think of the past for a moment. If you were in Sunday school as a young person, what do you remember best? I remember Miss Lyman. She was a dynamo for Christ. Certainly she taught doctrine and scripture. But more than that, she lived for Christ. Her enthusiasm was contagious. She came to Sunday school excited and prepared. I might not have understood everything she taught, but she was excited. She laughed. Her eyes sparkled when she talked about Jesus. I remember her promising to give a pocket-sized New Testament to anyone who could memorize 25 Bible promises. Each week, a different promise was taught. By the end of the year, anyone who had been in class regularly knew the promises and received a Bible. I remember how thrilled she was in giving those Bibles away. She had kept her promise to us. She gave each young person a Bible and a hug of congratulations.

I learned a lot about Christ from Miss Lyman. But more, I met Christ in her. Do you remember a teacher or youth worker like that? If so, celebrate! Give thanks! If not, shouldn't there be more teachers and youth workers like Miss Lyman?

Very often, young people receive their clearest images of Christ through the relationships they have with their teachers and youth workers. If we wait until young people are in junior or senior high to reach them for Christ, we may miss the opportunity completely. An insensitive teacher in preschool or an elementary class could turn a person off to Christ for years. A negative experience in Sunday school could cause a young person to drop out of church. Or, the young person might refuse to go to youth groups or Sunday school when the parents no longer force him or her to go.

Two key factors work together here for friendship evangelism in teaching and youth work. The first is recruiting—asking effective people to teach and work with youth. The second is training—equipping people with appropriate skills to work with youth.

In recruiting people to teach and work with youth, these qualities are important:

● a vital, personal faith in Christ—the person is excited, enthusiastic about Christ, the scriptures and Christian lifestyle;

● loves children or youth;

● has the gift of teaching and youth work—this gift is conveyed by the Holy Spirit (1 Corinthians 12:28; Ephesians 4:11);

● follows through on commitment—a teacher and youth worker need to be there, prepared, on time, whenever assigned to teach;

● is willing to learn and study—effective teachers and youth workers grow themselves through personal, spiritual discipline as well as the church's training program.

A word of caution when recruiting teachers: People who teach professionally may or may not make good Sunday school teachers or youth workers. They may feel like they need a break from a busy week of working with young people. Recruit church members who have the unique gift of making God's truths clear and simple for children and youth. Perhaps they feel a call to teach or work with young people in the church.

Effective teachers and youth workers build positive relationships with young persons. This is done through affirmation, caring and reaching out. Here are specific ways teachers and youth workers can build relationships:

1. Effective teachers and youth workers always look for ways to *affirm* youth. This goes beyond simple verbal affirmation, though positive statements such as "well done" and "great idea" are needed. Affirmation begins with the leaders immediately learning the names of all the youth. The teacher and youth worker should not use nicknames such as "honey" or "guy." They should call youth by the names they prefer. Put-downs are also out! The church needs to be the one place where young people can go and feel built up, not put down. The authority given for teaching and youth work is the same that Paul had in the early church, ". . . the authority which the Lord has given me for building up and not for tearing down" (2 Corinthians 13:10).

One Sunday morning, as I taught the high school class, I got into a put-down war with one of the students. He zapped me

37

with a great cut. I returned with a better put-down. The custom in the class was to try to outdo one another's sarcastic remarks. I thought it was cute—a way to relate to youth on their ground. Wrong! I'm sure that Kevin never heard another thing I said that Sunday. After class as I walked toward the sanctuary, he fired a parting shot. His put-down, however, was heard not only by me but also by his father. Kevin's father sternly scolded him for not showing respect to the minister. I learned something very important that Sunday. I could teach all I wanted about Christ's love, but unless I exemplified that love all the time—even in Sunday school—my words would be lost. I went back to working on building an affirming relationship with Kevin instead of playing the same, old put-down games he experienced at school, on the athletic teams, perhaps even at home. Sunday school is supposed to be different from some youth settings outside the church—it's to be a place where adults intentionally build youth up instead of putting them down.

2. Effective teachers and youth workers are *accepting*. Adolescence is a time of questioning. James Fowler examines some of the dimensions of doubt and questioning in puberty. In Fowler's research interviews, one 16-year-old youth reflected, "It really bothers me a lot because I don't know the answers and no one knows the answers, and I can't turn to anyone to get the answers—except to God, if there is a God. Maybe someday I'll get a vision from the Almighty!"[3]

Part of the invitation a teacher and youth worker extend to the young people is to allow them to question and search. To accept youth where they are and allow them to seek and question is vital to building relationships. Teachers often feel that they must be so prepared that they can answer every question. No amount of preparation will cover every question. When teachers and youth workers don't know the answer, it is best to be honest. To admit that one doesn't know and to invite the young person to join in the search for the answer is evangelism. Remember that Philip invited Nathanael to "Come and see." Mystery has a place in evangelism. Faith involves the unseen as well as the seen, the unknown as well as the known (Hebrews 11:1). Teachers who allow for mystery invite youth to search for Christ themselves, to delve deeper in prayer and meditation, to study the scriptures.

3. Effective teachers and youth workers *program for youth success.* Remember the story about Miss Lyman? Think about her techniques. She did everything possible to program for success so that the youth could learn the promises and receive the Bible. Sunday school and youth meetings are not places to embarrass youth by pointing out what they don't know. Following are potentially embarrassing moments and ways to avoid them:

● Youth are forced to go around the circle and read a passage of scripture out loud. The poor readers stumble over the words.

Remedy: Read passages in unison. Read some passages as cheers, responsive readings, or choral readings with small groups assigned to read different parts. You can even stage a shouting match between groups assigned to parts of a passage.

● Youth have to find a Bible passage when they don't know where to look. Not all youth come into a Sunday school class or youth meeting with the same educational background. Some know all the books in the Bible in order; others know few or none.

Remedy: Encourage those who don't know where passages are found to use the table of contents. Have extra Bibles in the room for those who are without. Use a contemporary translation so that the scriptures are easy to understand.

● Youth are required to say a sentence prayer. What about the youth who are uncomfortable with praying in front of a group?

Remedy: Have youth focus their prayer on a particular theme or idea. For example, "What is one thing you are grateful for today?" "What is one need someone in your family or one of your friends has—without naming the person?" "What is one way Christ might help you grow in this coming week?" The sharing also could be done with a prayer partner instead of with the entire group.

It is essential that teachers and youth workers plan ahead so that every assignment is programmed for success. All the materials need to be in the room. All the steps for implementing the lesson are thought out well in advance. Enough time is planned for the kids to complete the assignment. Youth are not put in situations that will be embarrassing.

4. Effective teachers and youth workers enable youth to *share with others.* Effective teachers and youth workers understand that they are not the only evangelists. Teachers who have to be center stage all the time may not be desirable recruits for working with children and youth. Teachers and youth workers who see others (youth as well as adults) as potential evangelists are more effective.

Young people are very effective witnesses in leading one another to Christ. Later in this book, we will focus on peer-evangelism training. This training is enhanced when youth have already been sharing with each other throughout the early Sunday school years. When children explore the scriptures and learn together, they reinforce understanding and faith. If the only relationships built in a group are between adults and youth, then many opportunities for learning and evangelism will be missed. As children and youth learn about faith and share ideas with each other, friendship evangelism begins to develop. They witness to one another through learning and sharing. This process is initiated by the teacher and youth worker. The more the youth share with one another, the more opportunities Christ has to work in their lives. This witnessing will take place when the teacher and youth worker implement one-to-one sharing, learning centers, small group discussions, and encourage questions and searching. Part of reaching our own is to allow them to reach each other.

TRAINING TEACHERS AND YOUTH WORKERS

Training for teachers and youth workers usually focuses on skills, techniques and content. Teachers or youth workers are viewed as conveyors of knowledge and wisdom. They may exercise authority by imposing their opinions and doctrine on passive youth who are told to sit still, shut up and learn. Experiential learning and relational Bible studies emerged with power and persuasiveness in the writings of Lyman Colemen, Keith Miller, Bruce Larson, Dennis Benson and J. David Stone. The power behind youth actively participating in the learning process is that both witness and invitation come from teacher, youth worker and student alike.

In the Faith at Work movement, William Clemmons provides insights into friendship evangelism:

Friendship working with youth combines **group building** with **content study** and does not major exclusively on inward-gazing or content-mastery ... Friendship working with youth builds on the creation of interpersonal relationships in which content ... speaks to each one where he is in his pilgrimage.[4]

Friendship evangelism gives the kids permission to form deep, meaningful relationships with their peers and the teacher or youth worker. These relationships give a deeper impact and credibility to the teacher's or youth worker's witness of the biblical content he or she is seeking to communicate.

In teacher and youth worker training, the instructors must teach techniques and illustrate behaviors that enhance positive relationships. The adult should become aware of how verbal and non-verbal behaviors affect both the learning process and the communication of the Gospel.

Following are a few pointers for organizing leadership training sessions:

1. Plan regular training sessions for teachers and youth workers. Continuity is an important aspect of a successful support group for adults working with youth.

2. During the training time, schedule group building activities for the teachers and youth workers. It is important to build community and cohesiveness among the leaders.

3. Pray for personal concerns as well as concerns about the young people.

4. Ask the teachers and youth workers to discuss any of their problems, conflicts or needs. This discussion may range from art supply needs to problems with handling a particularly disruptive teenager. Deal openly with the adults' concerns. Plan strategies for meeting those needs.

5. Utilize these three specific blocks of time during training sessions.

● **First 30 minutes**—group building; sharing needs, concerns and problems; coordinating dates and activities with the church calendar.

● **Next 30 minutes**—teaching techniques; practical ways to improve teaching skills. For example, using audio-visual equipment, leading relationship-building exercises, learning Bible study skills, planning sessions, etc.

● **Final 30 minutes**—spiritual disciplines. This is a time for feeding teachers and youth workers. Adult leaders should be involved in learning doctrine and applying it to their class settings and personal lives. Adults should be taught and encouraged in spiritual disciplines of study, prayer, meditation, worship, service, etc. Adults need to be nurtured in their own spiritual lives. Teachers and youth workers can't teach what they don't know.

At the sessions, present supplemental resources such as books, films, materials and ideas for the upcoming classes and activities. Concrete help with lesson planning adds a special incentive for attendance. But more than this, the leaders experience Christ in relationship to other adults.

Here are some specific behaviors to emphasize in leadership training. Role play the following situations:

● Walk into a noisy group of youth and angrily yell, "Sit down! Shut up! Everyone open your Bibles to 1 Corinthians 13. Our lesson today is on love."

Now ask the teacher and youth workers to describe the kinds of messages the youth could receive from the leader's behavior. What other ways could the leader have quieted the group? What did he or she communicate about the worth of youth? Did the adult embody the love written about in 1 Corinthians 13? Why or why not? Suggest these other ways to quiet the group:

● Walk into the room with suckers, distribute them and invite every student to start sucking on one.

● Immediately hand out Bibles and envelopes to everyone in the room. The Bible passage and first learning task have been written on a 3×5 card and placed inside each envelope. This message has been written on the outside of each envelope, "As soon as everyone in the room is QUIET, open this envelope. BUT, DO NOT OPEN UNTIL THERE IS SILENCE."

● Enter the room and talk to every student, call each by name, touch each person on the shoulder, offer a handshake or a hug (or even initiate a special handshake).

● Assign everyone a partner and give this assignment, "Share with your partner the greatest or the craziest thing that happened to you this week. Each of you has 30 seconds. I'll call time after one minute. Go."

These exercises encourage the leaders to creatively enter

into relationships with their youth at the beginning of the session. Now ask them to dream up other ways to start class.

In leadership training, the more specific we are in giving concrete ideas for building positive youth relationships, the more effective the adults will be in communicating the Gospel. Following are specific relationship-building ideas for leaders:

- attend a youth lock-in or retreat;
- volunteer to be a sponsor on a youth trip;
- send birthday cards to the young people;
- write notes of encouragement to the kids during exams, family problems, breakups with friends, or special events in which their achievements are recognized. Include brief scripture passages that encourage and build them up;
- occasionally sit with the youth during worship;
- attend special events at school or in the community—especially those events in which the young people are participating;
- plan a session or activity in the leader's home.

Our high school leaders met each Sunday afternoon in one of their homes to plan the lesson for next Sunday. They debriefed what had happened that very morning in class. They reflected on each young person's reactions, comments and needs and then prayed for the students. They planned and applied the next Sunday's lesson to the lives of the youth—tests, papers, dating, the big football game, the latest movie or rock hit. These teachers truly loved and cared for the young people; and the young people knew it.

The teachers decided to plan a special class for Palm Sunday. They wanted to have the class at one of their homes located close to the church. They made arrangements, publicized the event, and ordered small crosses for each young person.

On Palm Sunday, the young people met at the teacher's home. During the lesson, the teachers gave the students each a cross and told them that Christ gave his life for them. That class really touched the lives of many of those youth. They experienced Good Friday and Easter in a new and exciting way as they wore that cross in worship. Evangelism happened in that class. Not just on one Palm Sunday, but every Sunday those teachers gave themselves to the young people. The teachers reached out to the students, giving the students the desire to reach out to others.

One Easter the youth group members wanted to spread the joy of the risen Christ. They ordered small, colorful paper butterflies. During Sunday school and before the Easter worship service, the youth walked throughout the church and gave each person they met a butterfly and said, "He is risen. I have seen him." Without further comment they went to the next person. The people pinned the butterflies on their clothing. The impact of this simple witnessing act was tremendous.

Another Easter, the youth group members produced a "Jerusalem Times" newspaper. They wrote stories of the Crucifixion and Resurrection as if they were living in the first century. They printed the newspaper on newsprint and distributed copies to everyone at church on Easter Sunday.

In **Catching the Rainbow**, J. David Stone and I present a concept of group process which integrates both faith and leadership development.[5] The first step in developing a close-knit youth group is "telling our story." In his **Serendipity** materials, Lyman Coleman calls this "first base."[6] Young people telling their stories, relating experiences of their past week or month or years, builds a foundation for relationships that leads to feelings of belonging and community. When young people and their leaders look back at their lives, they can identify times when God was intimately working in their lives and times when they felt alienated from God.

Evangelism involves both telling how God acted historically in Christ to redeem man and how he acts personally to redeem each of us. Both stories are essential. A critical conversion point is to understand that God, in Christ, reconciled himself to the world and to us.

A teacher once gave our daughter **The Children's Living Bible**.[7] The teacher highlighted John 3:16 with a yellow marker. Also, by that verse the teacher inserted a special bookmark with our daughter's name. On close inspection, our daughter noticed that the word "world" was crossed out and her name was written in its place. That made a tremendous impression on our elementary-age daughter. First, the teacher had cared enough to give her a gift. Secondly, the teacher had affirmed that our daughter was personally loved by Christ. That love of Christ was driven home by the personal relationship between child and teacher.

Training for teachers and youth workers allows the adults to explore ways to deepen relationships with their young people, to build relationships between the teenagers, and to invite each young person to experience Christ through these relationships.

Relationships deepen most effectively when adults are vulnerable—when they risk sharing their stories, lives, successes and failures. Relationships deepen when young people hear each other's stories. They learn that others have the same problems. They discover ways to pray, to search for God's will and to experience his forgiveness.

In leadership training, it is important to understand intentional invitation. Intentional invitation is an adult being ever-prepared to ask young people to commit their lives to Christ. For example, a session can focus on the "down times" of living a Christlike life. One young person might share that the kids at school ridicule his going to church. In the course of the session, solutions can be discussed for coping with the ridicule. The leader should plan to set aside class time to discuss topics such as "taking the next step" or "deciding what Christ wants me to do." At the end of the class the leader can plan an activity to invite each young person to make a decision. For example, have a prayer time and allow the teenagers to ask for God's guidance in particular situations. Or, distribute pencils and 3×5 cards. Ask the participants to each write one goal for their spiritual growth. Each person will leave class having made a new or renewed commitment to follow Christ.

INTENTIONAL FRIENDSHIP EVANGELISM

One of the keys to friendship evangelism is the concept of "invitation," which we have just discussed. Invitation is deliberately including in every youth meeting a time for decision, commitment and affirmation of our Christian faith. Invitation is not making an altar call every youth meeting. Invitation can take many forms. Here are some simple exercises and worship moments that involve invitation. The exercises help the leaders plan for friendship evangelism.

Trust Fall
Divide the youth group members into pairs. Ask the taller

young person to stand behind the shorter one and place his or her hands on the shorter person's shoulders. Have the young people give their partners a gentle, soothing shoulder rub. Instruct the youth in front to close their eyes and the youth in back to drop their hands. Tell the youth in front that on the count of three they are to fall backward into the arms of their partner. Instruct the young people in back to move forward slightly so that they can easily catch their partner. The young people will laugh, giggle nervously and make crazy comments. Reassure everyone that those falling will be caught. Next say, "One, two, three . . . fall." Then, have the kids switch places and repeat the entire process.

This simple exercise teaches much about faith. Invariably, some youth fall quickly and with complete trust while others barely fall—stumbling backward and catching themselves.

The debriefing on this exercise embodies the nature of invitation. Have the young people discuss these questions:
- What did you feel right before you fell?
- What did you think as you were falling?
- What did you feel as you fell?
- Did you try to catch yourself or stop your fall? Why or why not?
- How is falling backward like trusting in God?
- How is trying to stop your fall like doubt?
- Can you doubt yet still have faith? Explain.

This exercise brings to mind a number of other questions and comparisons. As background text, use Matthew 14:22-33—Peter is walking on the water to Christ. Ask the young people to respond to these questions:
- If Christ were the one promising to catch you, would you fall? Explain.
- Do you believe that Christ would catch you? Why or why not?
- What is one thing you can do this week to exercise your trust and faith in Christ?

The Why Exercise

Divide the youth group members into pairs. Have the oldest go first, and begin a conversation by saying, "I believe in God." Have the partner ask, "Why?" The oldest one then gives whatever answer or reason comes to mind. Once the oldest has completed their statement, the partner again asks, "Why?" Again, the oldest replies with whatever comes to mind. Tell the group members that they have one minute for this dialogue. Assure them that it's okay if they exhaust all their answers before a minute is up. Ask for questions and then say, "Go."

When the minute is up, tell the partners to switch. Follow the same process for one minute. Then ask the group members these discussion questions:

- How did you feel when you were first asked to do this?
- How did you feel each time your partner asked, "Why?"
- Was this a difficult exercise? Why or why not?
- What word would you use to describe the process you just went through?

Some young people fear that they will not know what to say during this activity. They often express surprise at how much they are able to say. Some young people feel anger or frustration with the person asking, "Why?"

For background texts, use Luke 12:8 and Romans 10:9. Explain to the group members that they just experienced confession as well as witnessing. They are confessing what they believe about God and Christ and they are witnessing to their partners. Help them to see that they can witness simply to others about Christ. Discuss how they feel when other people at school have witnessed to them. What's effective? Do some come on too strong? Are some unloving in their witnessing? Encourage those who have verbalized their beliefs about Christ for the first time, to follow and grow in their faith in Christ.

The question that many adults ask is, "What about the visitors attending the youth group or the kids who aren't Christians?" The fact that those teenagers are there indicates they have some interest or curiosity in Christ. A Search Institute survey indicated that 88 percent of young adolescents had some, or much, interest in "finding out what it means to be a Christian."[8] For some youth, this exercise is the first time they verbalize some of their beliefs and feelings about God. It is a first step in trusting Christ. We have yet to do this exercise and have a young person say nothing. It's both interesting and surprising, for the leader and the young people, to hear their answers.

A Letter to Christ

One of the most effective invitational tools for young people is letter writing. I often end a program, camp or retreat with a time of silence. I ask the participants to reflect on what the program has meant to them. Then, I ask them to write a letter to Christ, telling him how they feel about him and asking him for what they need. The participants seal and self-address the envelopes. A few weeks, or even months, after the letter is written, I mail the letters to the young people. They reread their letters to Christ which serve as a renewal of their commitment to him.

Ron Hutchcraft, a Youth for Christ area coordinator, gives a sample outline for letters to Christ.

> Write a letter. To whom? To Jesus! This will help him (the young person) begin the process of communicating with the Person he has just come to know. That letter can have five key paragraphs beginning with these phrases:
> 'I love you . . .'
> 'Thank you . . .'
> 'I'm sorry . . .'
> 'Please . . .'
> 'I promise . . .'[9]

Invitation Questions

Invitation is an awareness of the necessity of commitment. Youth as well as adults can set specific, concrete goals for spiritual growth. There are times when we make the Christian life too easy. We fail to ask for significant commitment. Invitations that can be processed by writing, praying or talking to a partner are:

- The next step I need to take is . . .
- Right now is a time in my life when . . .
- One behavior that I need to correct is . . .
- A way I can show my love for Christ at school (or at home, or to my parents, or to one of my friends) is . . .
- The 10 strengths that God has given me are . . .
- My most destructive attitude that God and I need to work on this coming week is . . .
- One thing that keeps me from giving my all to Christ is . . .
- God expects me to . . .

Beyond invitation in a program, worship, retreat or camp setting is creating an atmosphere of trust, acceptance and open sharing within a group. This happens when young people are encouraged to share with one another, build one-to-one and small group relationships and become a community of close-knit friends in Christ. One way to conceptualize a youth ministry with this type of atmosphere is through the following chart:[10]

YOUTH MINISTRY PROCESS CHART

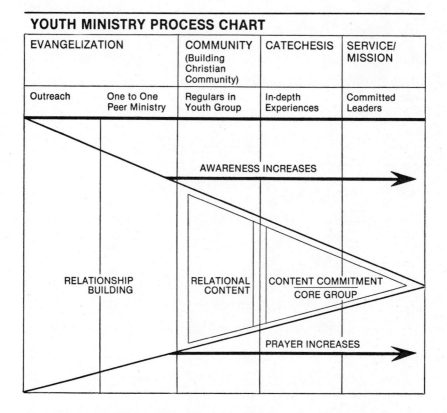

EVANGELIZATION		COMMUNITY (Building Christian Community)	CATECHESIS	SERVICE/ MISSION
Outreach	One to One Peer Ministry	Regulars in Youth Group	In-depth Experiences	Committed Leaders

AWARENESS INCREASES

RELATIONSHIP BUILDING — RELATIONAL CONTENT — CONTENT COMMITMENT CORE GROUP

PRAYER INCREASES

As indicated in this chart, evangelism is strongest in the midst of personal relationships. As those relationships grow and deepen, youth find that Christ is both meeting their needs and causing them to become more aware of the needs of others. Thus, service, prayer and awareness grow as youth mature spiritually.

This is dynamic theory. But, is there a practical model for experiencing this kind of friendship evangelism in a youth group or Sunday school class? A number of youth groups have used a model similar to the following one.

Intensive Care Units

Leaders set up this activity and make a commitment to provide leadership in the Intensive Care Units (ICUs). The process is simple. The youth group is divided into small groups of five or six young people and one leader (the leader could be an adult or teenager). Before the first ICU meeting, the leaders meet to set up the groups which are equally made up of males and females. They should try to break up the normal cliques within the youth group. Some youth in the ICUs know each other well, others are essentially strangers. The leader of each group agrees beforehand to:

- be very regular in attendance to youth meetings,
- call the ICU members or talk with them at school once a week,
- make a special effort to write or telephone absentees,
- pray daily for the ICU members,
- befriend any new ICU member.

Sometimes the ICUs may only meet for five minutes during a designated time in the youth meeting or class session. At other times, they meet for a longer period. Following is a sample format for sharing in an ICU:

1. The leader shares first.
2. The leader asks everyone to share something great that happened last week. For example:

- One way God blessed me last week was . . .
- I saw God at work in my life in . . .
- The best part of my week was . . .

3. The leader asks everyone to share something not so good that happened last week. For example:

- One of the worst things that happened last week was . . .
- Something I'd like to forget about last week is . . .
- If I could change last week, I would . . .

4. The leader tells the ICU members that they don't have to share and may pass if they wish.
5. The leader asks for prayer needs. For example:

- One thing I need you to pray for this week is . . .
- This week I need your prayers to face . . .
- A friend of mine needs your prayer in . .

After doing this for a while, the leaders will generate their own lead thoughts for sharing. At times, the entire ICU simply may want to sit, hold hands and pray silently. At other times, the ICU may leave the youth room to share or even to sing a chorus.

Another aspect of the ICUs is the incorporation of visitors or new youth group members. The first time a new person comes, the youth minister (adult volunteer or youth group leader) assigns that new person to an ICU. Very often, if that person has come with a friend or knows someone well in a particular ICU, he or she is assigned to that small group. The leader explains how the ICU works and invites that visitor to share or pass, as he or she feels comfortable. That new young person automatically has a group of friends—they are never alone or treated like an outsider.

The ICU leaders also know to contact new people during the following week and invite them back to the youth group. As the ICU grows closer, new dynamics begin to emerge. The ICU leaders encourage ICU members to call absent or new youth. The ICU may develop prayer partners within the small group. During the week, the partners may phone, visit or pray together. The ICU members also remember birthdays and special occasions. The ICU leaders encourage the group members to lead or start the sharing time.

Usually, the same people stay together within the ICUs for at least two to three months and often for a semester. Then the leaders shuffle all the members to form new groups so that different people can grow closer. Because of ICUs, one youth group I worked with grew in number from just a few to over 100 in an 18-month period. The members became excited about growing spiritually with one another. Friends who were brought to the youth group immediately felt included and needed. They desired to know more about this Christ, who knit youth together so closely in love and caring. What happens within ICUs is what Paul wrote about the Colossians, ". . . we have heard of your faith in Christ Jesus and of the love which you have for all the saints . . ." (Colossians 1:4).

Reaching our own youth involves every Christian in the congregation—teachers, youth workers, pastors, congregational leaders, members and youth themselves. When we intensify our training efforts, plan for invitation and build Christlike relationships, we will celebrate a harvest. Youth within the church will form eternal relationships with Jesus Christ. And they will begin reaching out to lead other youth to Christ.

THE PASTOR

Initially, pastors build relationships with young people through worship. His or her relationships with youth enable invitation within worship to become real and concrete. Not all congregations have an altar call or invitation built into the order of worship. Yet, a formal altar call is not the only method of invitation. Invitation comes through music, the sermon, the Eucharist or Holy Communion, prayer and other parts of the worship order. In this section, we will explore ways the pastor can be sensitive to friendship evangelism in worship.

First, let's discuss the formal invitation or altar call. At a specified time in some settings of worship, the minister or priest invites people to respond to the call of Jesus Christ. That invitation may sound something like this, "If any people desire to make Jesus Christ their personal Lord and Savior, they are invited to come forward during the singing of the invitation hymn." The minister's preparation of both youth and adults in relating to those who come forward is critically important. The minister should equip both adults and youth to counsel with those coming forward and to maintain a relationship after the altar call. Here's a model of friendship evangelism utilizing an altar call.

I received an invitation to keynote a large youth assembly in Pennsylvania. The place, times and process were set. Yet, their last request intrigued me. "On Saturday evening, you are to give an altar call after the keynote." They wanted more than a keynoter, more than a program, more than a guest speaker—they wanted an evangelist!

Certainly I knew about altar calls. Each Sunday after the sermon, I gave others an invitation to accept Jesus Christ. Keynoting youth conventions seemed a different proposition. My style was to share stories with a biblical point, to involve youth in the sharing of their own stories and lives and to focus on inner spiritual growth. To evangelize wasn't my style, I rationalized.

Everything went well during my initial sessions at the assembly. I delayed my plans for the altar call until the last moment. "Perhaps the Lord will give me tremendous insight into what I should do after I get to know the youth at the convention," I thought. But, no insight came. Saturday afternoon finally arrived and I was unprepared. After the afternoon session, a group of adults asked, "How are you going to handle the altar call tonight?" I had to say and do something, so I asked for their help.

For the next 30 minutes we discussed ideas. The insight I had been searching for was simple and biblical. Everyone bubbled with anticipation.

The setting for the evening was tough. I had expected a situation similar to the earlier sessions which included a massive hall, movable chairs and interpersonal sharing. For the evening session, we met in a church sanctuary complete with fixed pews, no air conditioning, and a pulpit that was six feet or more away from the young people. Nevertheless, I tried my best to speak. The heat almost put everyone to sleep, including me. Then it came—the invitation, the altar call. All speakers wonder at that moment. Will anyone respond? What if no one comes forward? Yet, responses to the call don't depend on speakers—the responses depend on the Holy Spirit working in people's lives.

Slowly, one came forward, then another, and then many. Excitement increased. The adults who had helped plan the altar call came forward to assist. For each young person there was an adult, a witness, a friend.

Something else exciting happened. Friends of those at the altar also came forward. People hugged each other, cried, spoke words of affirmation, and offered support. Friends were leading friends to Christ.

After the closing prayer, the adults asked the youth who came forward:

● What do you need to say to Christ?
● What do you most want to do right now?
● Will you do it?

Some of the youth needed to profess their faith in Jesus Christ. Others struggled with deep, difficult decisions. Still others needed to share a problem, a temptation, a sense of guilt, a desire for forgiveness. One-to-one, person-to-person, youth were hearing and responding to the Good News. The real evangelists of the evening were the adults the youth knew and trusted.

Throughout the sanctuary, small groups formed. Young people and adults reached out to one another. More teenagers responded to Christ in the pews than before the altar. The adults had been instructed, "If you see others really wrestling with something, go to them at the end of the service and ask them if they want to talk." People were sensitive to what was happening around them. Instead of simply walking out, they reached out to others.

As people were talking throughout the sanctuary, I moved down a side aisle. A young guy walked toward me. Tears were streaming down his face. His whole body trembled with sobs. Somehow, the adult from his group hadn't seen him or was with another person. He was alone. He must have played football and thought I was the ball. Towering over me, he grabbed me, held on as tightly as possible, and cried. Finally, he spoke, "I missed it. It's too late to go up front."

We sat down in a nearby pew and I simply said, "It's never too late. You didn't miss anything. God doesn't need an altar call to work in your life. What do you need to say to God right now?" He shared his need and his story. We talked for almost 30 minutes. He needed a friend who would listen. Then he accepted Christ and we prayed together.

Each adult had been prepared to pray with each youth after a decision was made. Then each youth was asked to write the decision on a piece of paper, put that into an envelope, and self-address the envelope. After a parting hug, handshake or word of assurance, the adult took the envelope home and did four things:

- contacted the youth's pastor about the decision,
- prayed for the youth,
- mailed a note or called the young person just to "touch base" during the next week,
- mailed the note to the youth as a reminder of that important decision.

Notice. Plans were made. People were prepared to reach out to others wanting to respond to Christ. Proclamation—sharing the Good News about Jesus Christ—was there. All of these things are important but the key is this: Friends can lead friends to Christ.

It's important for the pastor to plan for other youth and adults to participate in the evangelism process during the worship. Friendship evangelism begins with the pastor's sensitivity to the needs and concerns of the youth in his or her congregation.

The most effective way to build a positive relationship with youth is a ministry of presence. Having a relationship means "being there." One minister said that he cultivated relationships with his youth by attending the first night of every retreat. (He could not stay for the whole weekend because of his responsibilities on Sunday morning.) The night he attended, he participated with the youth in all that was planned. He didn't lead anything—he was simply there. So, if there were games the first night, he played. If a shaving cream fight broke out late at night between cabins, he was in the middle of it. He demonstrated a real interest and concern for the youth by "being there." Then on Saturday morning he would head back home.

I found other ways to be there. On Sunday evenings, I would periodically drop in on one of the youth group meetings. While I had no program responsibilities, I would participate in their activities. I shared with them, heard what was happening at school, and saw the youth group in action.

Another place for "being there" was at snack suppers. We held snack suppers once a week before youth group meetings. The church bought the supplies, parents made the meals, and the kids paid a minimal fee. We ate food such as pizza, tacos and hamburgers. It was wonderful to sit there and listen to all the latest news and happenings with the teenagers. They enjoyed seeing me around. If I happened to miss a supper, they would ask where I had been and if I would be able to attend the following week.

One high schooler really made an impression on me. He was having a tough time at school and relating to his parents. Sometimes, I dropped by to talk with him after school; at other times, I called him on the phone to see how things were going. Eventually I counseled with both him and his parents. Our relationship was building. Some difficult situations emerged. He had to live in a juvenile center for a while. From time to time, I went to visit. The relationship deepened. Then a life-threatening surgery was necessary. He entered a hospital which was 60 miles away from the church. A few youth group members called him and I visited with him occasionally. We talked seriously about life, death and faith in Christ. The key to sharing with him about Jesus Christ came in our friendship. I had been there for him in the good times and the bad. Because of our rapport, he was willing to listen.

He did fine in surgery. When he was dismissed from the hospital, the youth group members and I visited him at his home. We tried to "be there" when he needed us.

Some of the concrete steps a pastor can take to build positive relationships with youth are:

1. Be present at some youth events and happenings.

2. Drop in on snack suppers and youth classes or meetings.

3. Lead an occasional program, study or discussion.

4. Teach a youth class for a month or a quarter just to stay in touch.

5. Visit youth. They are often left out of general pastoral ministry. More than likely, elderly members, visitors, ill members or inactive adults are called upon. Minister of finance and administration at Dallas' Lovers Lane United Methodist Church, Kennon L. Callahan, suggests that ministers should spend "one hour in pastoral visitation each week for every minute you preach on Sunday morning."[11] If a minister made that many visits weekly, the youth would certainly be a part of pastoral visitation.

These basic steps would make the minister's call for commitment much more effective in reaching youth. The pastor also should address the needs of youth in the sermon. That can happen only when the pastor spends time with them, and when he or she becomes aware of youth culture. Here are some ways to be more sensitive.

1. Read contemporary youth magazines such as Rolling Stone, Teen, Seventeen, or Christian youth magazines such as Buzz, GROUP Members Only and Campus Life.

2. Talk regularly to junior and senior high school teachers and counselors about the youth culture.

3. Listen to the popular rock music that kids listen to. Ask them what radio stations they listen to and spend some time hearing what they hear.

4. Visit the local junior or senior high school. From time to time, eat lunch with your young people. Observe what's going

on at the schools.

5. Volunteer to chaperon some school functions, drive the school team to games or simply go to different school activities.

6. Coach or chaperon community youth programs.

7. Drop in to some of the night spots frequented by youth in your community. See where they go for entertainment and fun. Watch some of the movies they enjoy.

8. Visit department stores and discover the popular fashions for youth. Ask the store clerks about current youth fashions.

In sermons, mention a few of the facts you learned through your observations and involvement to establish some credibility with the youth. Once a pastor establishes credibility and builds relationships, sharing the Gospel becomes a more viable possibility with youth.

The pastor also needs to find ways to include youth in the worship service. Listen to their critique of worship. While worship cannot be tailored to meet just youth needs, those who plan the worship service need to provide music and liturgy that enable youth as well as adults to focus on God. One way to involve youth is to include them on the worship-planning committee. Another way is to include youth in the worship service itself. Encourage them to read the scriptures, lead prayers, give a children's sermonette, sing in a youth choir or ensemble, give the announcements or plan a youth Sunday.

Another point of contact is through confirmation or pastor's classes. Learning content is the only focus in many pastor's classes, evangelism curricula and confirmation materials. Learning the content of the scriptures and the Good News is essential. But, content isn't the only important dimension. The pastor should actively build relationships with youth or classes may become pedantic exercises on a superficial level. A relationship with Jesus Christ is not only taught, it's caught. The pastor is a role model of a Christian lifestyle. Christ's presence and seeking love is incarnated in the relationships that a pastor has with young people.

There are several ways that a pastor can enrich a class. Each year, one pastor takes his confirmation students on a retreat. He personally becomes involved for an entire weekend or week, witnessing and sharing.

Another pastor enhances his class by having one-on-one visits with his students over a three-month term. During those visits, he focuses on the concerns and questions of each individual. He is personally involved with each young person. The class members then believe the pastor when he or she says, "If you were the only person on earth, Christ would have given his life for you." Through individual attention, the pastor reinforces God's love, which gives dignity and self-worth to every young person. Individual attention builds the class members' self-esteem and satisfies their deep hunger for meaningful relationships.

Ministers need to give special consideration to older adolescents. Confirmation or pastor's classes are more effective when junior and senior high youth are grouped separately. Some churches put all adolescents who haven't been confirmed or who haven't accepted Christ in the same class. Older youth, particularly senior high students, resist going to a confirmation or pastor's class with junior high or younger students. One more effective way for a pastor to share Christ with an older teenager is to meet with him or her individually for a number of sessions discussing the Gospel and going over confirmation materials.

Once again, one of the most important factors in effective evangelism is the relationship a pastor builds with the young people in his or her church. Pastor "friends" lead "youth" friends to Christ.

JUNIOR HIGHERS

All of the concepts presented in this book can be used with junior highers. However, we must take into consideration the developmental level of early adolescents along with the behaviors they normally exhibit.

When adapting the programs and exercises in this book for junior highers, remember these basic principles:

● **Plan for shorter attention spans.** Program 70 percent of the time for high-energy interaction and participatory learning. Program 30 percent of the time for more content-focused activities. Senior highers will often devote more time to serious discussions and interaction than junior highers.

● **Expect junior highers to think concretely.** Much of the ability to think abstractly begins to emerge in later adolescence. For example, during one exercise junior highers were asked to choose a small stone from an assortment of stones. Then, each was asked to share with a partner how they thought that stone represented the faith of Peter—the rock. Many of the junior highers giggled, and said they thought the exercise was silly. They ended up throwing the rocks at one another rather than sharing their reflections. On the other hand, when this activity was presented to senior highers, they spent a significant amount of time thinking of all the analogies between a rock and Peter.

● **Junior highers work quickly.** I have been amused at some junior high Sunday school curricula. The teachers are instructed to allow 15 minutes for a certain learning activity. Junior highers zoom through the activity in five minutes, leaving the teacher grasping for another exercise to fill the time.

● **Junior highers are curious and eager to learn.** Often senior highers see themselves as more sophisticated and more knowledgeable. Junior highers more readily accept information and are eager to explore new ideas. They usually are more open and candid about feelings and questions. They haven't yet learned all the game playing that senior highers have.

● **Give detailed instructions.** Of course, with all youth activities, instructions need to be clear and specific. Although senior highers may fill in the gaps, junior highers need to know every detail of your expectations. Once I was demonstrating the Trust Fall at a retreat for over 200 junior highers. I thought I had covered every detail. I had been very specific in explaining that the "behind" partner should catch the one falling. If that point is unclear, some junior higher will let the falling person hit the ground just to see what will happen. So, I chose a strong, tall junior high boy to stand behind me and catch me. I was demonstrating the exercise. However, I failed to explain at what point I wanted him to catch me. While I talked, he moved about five feet behind me and kneeled down. Of course, I expected to be caught after falling about two feet. With complete trust, I fell. After falling about two feet, I started to pray. After three feet, I knew I was going to die! Fortunately, he caught me about a foot off the floor. From then on, I gave very detailed instructions to junior highers about every exercise.

● **Junior highers are more shy about touch.** They often will giggle, joke or even refuse to hold hands with one another. Determine what level of touching your group is most comfortable with.

One of the exciting things about junior highers and friendship evangelism is that they are usually much more eager than older students to invite their friends to youth group and church. Plan interesting programs and fun gatherings to give your junior highers an opportunity to invite their friends. Encourage your junior highers to reach out to others who may not have a lot of friends at school. This way they will begin early to learn that Christ's love is not just for the popular kids, but for everyone.

Chapter Three

Reaching Beyond Our Own

*H*ow do we reach out to unchurched and non-Christian youth? As we discussed in Chapter 1, *all* young people hunger for deep relationships and spirituality. This includes non-Christians as well as Christians; unchurched as well as churched. In early adolescence, peer influence increases while parental influence begins to diminish. Early adolescence becomes a time for seeking independence from parental control. From fifth to ninth grade, the desire to "make my own decisions" increases dramatically. Peer influence in that decision-making process becomes very significant. The Search Institute study on early adolescence reported, ". . . three dynamics occur between the 5th and 9th grade: peer influence increases, parent influence decreases, and parents remain the *strongest* of the two influences even though parent influence declines during the period of early adolescence."[1]

Essential to this period of life are supportive networks of friends. Youth help one another form values and make life-shaping decisions. If the parents of unchurched youth are not Christians, then a vital witnessing link is absent. It becomes crucial that Christian friends reach out to their non-Christian friends with the Good News. The models of Philip and Nathanael (John 1:43-50), and Peter and Andrew (John 1:35-42) exemplify evangelism. *It takes a friend to lead a friend to Christ.*

Let's look at a secular example of peer influence. In countless studies of drug abuse, young people are swayed by friends or siblings. A close friend or sibling introduces another to the drug. Peer pressure is powerful! Why not allow this reality to work for good and not evil? It is exciting to explore how youth can influence their friends for Christ, for Christian values, for Christian community, and for building one another up instead of tearing one another down.

Chapter 2 emphasized the importance of the church culti-vating friendship evangelism in settings such as Sunday school, worship, youth groups and visitation. The church must also cultivate within the youth the desire to evangelize. Reach-ing non-Christian youth with the Gospel sounds basic and fun-damental, yet not all churches "walk" the way they "talk." Some churches profess that witnessing is great, but when non-Christian kids begin coming, they are unprepared. Visitors may not be used to the church. They may not know how to act in worship services or youth meetings. They may not have the same morals or manners. Some parents may complain that these outsiders are "corrupting" their kids. Others may be concerned that additional members will mean that more money will be needed for programs and events. The church youth may resent unchurched kids "barging in" on their group. The youth group and church usually can handle one or two unchurched visitors, but what if five, or 10, or more come at the same time? Is the church willing to pay the price for reaching out to unchurched young people?

Burt was a likable, but unconventional, youth group mem-ber. His parents were active members of the church and com-mitted believers. Burt confessed Christ, but he also possessed some qualities that many youth in our group questioned. What-ever the current fad, Burt quickly tried it. He asked probing, intelligent questions about faith, but he didn't fit into the win-some, all-American Christian mold. Curiously enough, he felt comfortable in the youth group and also invited many of his school friends; not just one or two, but often seven or more. Burt's friends became very active in both Sunday school and the youth group. Some of their behavior and language was un-acceptable to other youth, and parents alike. Parents began to voice concern that this group of outsiders was having a nega-tive influence on their children. Youth group volunteers were undecided over how to discipline and handle this sizable clique. Burt's friends came to have a good time, and more. They seemed to be seeking for answers to their questions. They definitely needed Christian values and Christ in their lives. Yet, how much risk does a church take in exposing its own youth group to outside influence? Some of the youth complained that Burt and his friends were not spiritual enough, while others felt that they wouldn't take their fair share of responsibility for group tasks.

The problems arising from this situation could have been anticipated. Many youth group members bring their friends, yet very few churches have prepared the adults or youth to fellowship the unchurched youth. Somehow, osmosis is supposed to occur. When unchurched kids come to youth meetings, trips or retreats they are expected to speak the right language and to behave like believers. Isn't that assumption both askew and naive? If unchurched youth use vulgarity at home or school, then wouldn't they use it at church as well? They have no concept of the language or behavioral taboos in church, much less the ethical system of the Gospel. If the church wants to reach unchurched youth, it must be willing to pay the price. The cost involves risk and many other factors. Christian youth and adults should be properly trained. Attitudes of deep caring and firm commitment to Christian values are critical.

This chapter presents a systematic approach for reaching the unchurched, wherein the fourth chapter, practical and effective programs for reaching out are discussed. Why in this order? Let's suppose that a church youth group becomes exciting. It is a fun place to be. Church youth develop deep relationships with one another and build a solid faith in Christ. Everything is working. Youth are so excited about Christ and their group that they enthusiastically invite their friends to join in the activities. The youth group successfully plans a youth center, sports day, after-school program or street dance. What happens when the unchurched, non-Christian youth attend? Who is equipped to share the Gospel with them? Who is prepared for "street" attitudes and behaviors? Who answers their questions about the Christian faith? Who discusses with them the strict rules on the retreat? Who is prepared for young people who may not respect church property or members?

Models for reaching unchurched, non-Christian youth are

only effective if certain attitudes exist in the church, and if both youth and adults are equipped and trained for reaching out. Once we have established the necessary attitudes and how to attain them, we can explore specific training models for friendship evangelism. Jesus provided the foundation for such a process. First, he worked on the "attitudes for being" (Matthew 5) with his followers. He also spent three years teaching and preparing his own disciples to proclaim the Gospel. In the next section, we will discuss the necessary attitudes our own young people need to develop in order to reach non-Christians.

EVANGELISTIC ATTITUDES

Three critical attitudes must be present to effectively evangelize to the unchurched: inclusion, willingness to risk, desire to meet their needs.

Inclusion is an important attitude. One church's marquee stated, "We reserve the right to accept anyone here." Another church printed in its bulletin, "The 350 ministers of this church are here to serve you." Are we inclusive or exclusive in our attitudes? Youth are turned off by churches which appear to be exclusive, "elect clubs."

We had moved to Colorado and had been visiting a particular church for a few weeks when suddenly our foster daughter didn't want to go. At first she was embarrassed to tell me why. Then she bluntly said, "Well, all the kids there seem stuck up. Besides, they all wear dresses. I don't feel right in my jeans." She had never had an expansive wardrobe. In fact, her mainstay in fashion was jeans. Dresses were not her style.

Now some adult who reads this may think, "That kid shouldn't let something so silly as wearing dresses keep her from going to church." But, no matter what we think, it will not change the way she or other kids feel.

Churches erect all kinds of barriers to unchurched youth. Some churches place restrictions on who can or can't come to events. One congregation pays half of the cost for young people to go on trips and retreats. But, the catch is that the young person, or the parents, must be members of the church. Imagine how that unchurched visitor feels—the church kids pay $25, but she will have to pay $50. That builds an unnecessary barrier. Of course, if the youth are doing a fund-raising project to go on a trip, only those youth who work should share in the money raised. But, *all* who work should share. And, if the youth who aren't church members work, they should share equally with the church youth. If a young person hasn't worked on the fund raiser, yet genuinely wants to go on the trip and is willing to pay the full cost, let him or her go. Some youth and adults will complain that such an inclusive attitude isn't fair. But isn't God's love (agape) unconditional?

Our junior high group in Texas worked hard for over 18 months to raise money for a trip to Disney World and a spiritual life retreat at a beachside-conference center in Florida. At the last minute, one of the girls in our group invited a friend. Her friend did not attend church. She hadn't participated in any of the preparations or projects. As it happened, there were a few seats left on the bus. The friend was willing to pay her way. The youth council and I accepted her reservation. Some of the youth group members were really unhappy that this outsider was going.

The trip was a beautiful experience. The friend fit in well with the Bible studies, sharing times and recreational activities. Years later, I met that girl at a church event. She came up and said, "Remember me?" Her face was familiar but I couldn't quite place her. "I went on that bus trip to Florida. Soon after we got back, my family moved to another town. But something happened to me on that trip. I started going to church in my new town without my parents and made some new Christian friends. I met Christ there. It all started with that trip. Thanks for letting me go."

I believe that when we are centered and focused on Christ, young people will be drawn to him through us. We should never deprive anyone the opportunity to meet him by refusing to allow them to go on a trip, retreat or event.

Remember the story of the workers in the vineyard (Matthew 20)? Some hired help who began working at the end of the day were paid the same wage as those who had started in the morning. The workers who had come in the early morning complained about the unfairness. That parable could have been a youth group. Youth will usually complain when one young person gets to go on a trip at the last minute, when others have worked for months to go. Yet, if friendship evangelism becomes a reality, the young people will set a greater goal: to reach out to others with Christ's love. Youth will be excited to share the Good News with new youth on a trip. When young people cultivate this kind of attitude, friendship evangelism has taken hold.

Another story relates to this. In one church I served, we had very active church athletic teams. Our team coaches were skilled in their sports and also in the Christian life. We insisted that our coaches put Christ first in their coaching, not winning. I wondered at times when I observed other church teams play if they ever had heard the Gospel. Coaches would cuss, scream, and verbally abuse their players, the opponents or referees. I believe that the Gospel is compromised, and a negative witness is made by such behavior, in church leagues. So, as part of our evangelistic strategy, we recruited Christian coaches who built up players and didn't tear them down. These coaches could share the love of Christ as easily as the rules of the game.

A church rule was that young people had to attend Sunday school and worship regularly in order to play on the teams. One high schooler, whose parents belonged to the church, never came to anything. But, he signed up to play on the church basketball team. He had just missed the cut for playing on the varsity team at school. We decided to let this boy play on the team. His need to play competitive basketball was met. He found inclusion and acceptance at church. He started to come to the youth group meetings after basketball season ended. Christ became the center of his life, and later, as a young adult, he became one of the most popular church league coaches. Other youth began to meet Christ through him.

I visited a church in California that had a very subtle way of excluding young people. It refused to provide a comfortable, good meeting space for them. The youth room was very small, cramped and obviously not decorated by the young people. Only a handful of church kids participated in the program. I asked them why they never invited their friends to church. The answer was simple. "We would be embarrassed to bring our friends. There's nothing here for them." Although that church had just built a multimillion-dollar sanctuary—it was built to meet the needs of adults, not the needs of youth. The one time the young people were permitted to play an indoor game in the fellowship hall, a light fixture had been broken. A policy was then enforced that banned the kids from using that room. Evangelism suffers when priorities are placed on policies rather than on people. We become more concerned with what we possess than with the one who should possess us.

Here's a checklist for the attitude of inclusion. If you can answer "yes" to most of these questions, your church and youth program are well on their way toward reaching out to include unchurched young people.

● Does our church budget support both member youth and their unchurched friends?

● Do we permit unchurched kids to participate in all of our programs?

● Is the youth facility or room in our church inviting and comfortable for all young people who may come?

● Do we have any rules or policies that encourage unchurched youth to attend?

● Do we avoid singling unchurched youth out in any of our policies or programs in such a way that they would be embarrassed?

● Are the subtle, non-verbal messages we give out encouraging church members to bring their non-Christian friends?

The second necessary attitude for effective evangelism is a *willingness to risk*. Talking to the woman in Samaria was risky. Stopping the stoning of an adulteress was risky. Challenging the religious leaders of the day was risky. Casting out demons and raising the dead was risky. Eating and drinking with the dredges of society was risky. Christ lived radical commitment, ultimate risk. Following Christ is risky.

Perhaps we want to be known as nice Christians. Nice Christians aren't disturbed or disturbing. One speaker at a youth conference reflected, "Christians are in the business of comforting the afflicted and afflicting the comfortable." Asking Christians to be willing to risk, requires both sincerity and commitment. Pastors, associates and youth ministers need to prepare their congregation for the risks, if evangelism is to be taken seriously. Unchurched youth may come; their attitudes and behaviors may be undesirable from the congregation's perspective. Property, policy and people may get hurt. Risky, isn't it? In the next chapter, I will describe a model youth center and after-school program for evangelistic outreach to the unchurched.

Another way to illustrate risk-taking evangelism is to talk about money. Spending money is always risky. The first time I discovered this was early in my ministry when I took the new year's youth budget to the finance committee. I planned for the costs involved in maintaining, as well as expanding, the current youth program. I learned that churches are often looking for ways to cut or reduce their budgets, not expand. To budget for "potential" youth group members seemed a waste of money to some committee members. Yet, if I did not plan for growth, then I might run out of budgeted funds halfway through the year. Youth groups often fail to grow because they don't plan to grow. They budget so miserly that growth becomes an economic liability. So, if new kids come, they deplete the amount of funds that would have been spent on the participating church youth. A limited youth budget is often a message to church members, "Don't bring your friends, we can't afford them."

A second financial consideration is appropriate to mention here. A youth program that is costly for members to participate in may discourage attendance. If the members, or their parents, have to pay for every activity, week after week, the ministry becomes too costly and thus exclusively for the wealthy. One church has a dynamic youth program on Sunday mornings and uses its evening fellowship time for recreational activities. Each week there's pizza, bowling, swimming, miniature golf or skating. Each week the parents, or kids, have to come up with money to participate. Somewhere, evangelism gets lost in the shuffle for money.

Growth is costly and risky. A congregation needs to be educated to the costs and risks involved in reaching out to new people. When a congregation wants to implement an outreach program, meetings should be scheduled well in advance to carefully plan the necessary strategies and costs. Through leadership and sermons, the entire congregation should be educated in the full scope of the evangelistic outreach. Enthusiastically moving into an outreach program, and then having to cut back, really damages the credibility of the Gospel with unchurched youth. Following is a step-by-step approach to weighing the congregation's willingness to risk:

1. Far in advance of any major evangelistic outreach to un-

churched youth, plan a timeline. Start six months, a year or even further ahead to plan and prepare.

2. Carefully budget the cost based on how many youth will be reached within a year, and how much it will cost to run the program with the new people involved.

3. Structure a thorough training program for all young people and adults involved in the outreach program. Be certain to equip them with the biblical background necessary for effective witnessing. Also, include tips for weekly management of program details. If you plan to open up an after-school program, here are some examples of program details:

- Who does the shopping for snacks?
- Who opens and closes the building?
- Who recruits volunteers?
- Who handles the money?

4. Plan periodic meetings with church leaders and at least one comprehensive meeting for the congregation to discuss the outreach and the risks involved. Define:

- purpose,
- objectives,
- strategies,
- timeline,
- training process,
- on-going costs, and
- hoped-for results of the outreach.

Get approval from the appropriate decision-making groups in your church each step of the way. Continually communicate the plans and progress.

5. Openly discuss the risks. From the start, seek to anticipate surprises and problems. Establish a process for handling surprises once the evangelistic outreach is set in motion.

6. Involve everyone in in-depth prayer throughout the planning and implementation of the outreach. God's Spirit will give a boldness to a congregation seeking to share the Gospel with unchurched youth. Pray for wisdom and boldness. Read Acts 4:29.

The third necessary attitude for effective outreach is a *desire to meet needs.* In the late '70s, I attended the Institute for Successful Church Leadership held at the Crystal Cathedral in Garden Grove, California. Dr. Robert Schuller, the pastor of that congregation, discussed growth principles. A few people may disagree with the marketing growth techniques that Schuller uses. Yet, several of his insights are valuable. Some of the now familiar concepts caught my attention. "Find a need and meet it; find a hurt and heal it." Dr. Schuller reflected that most churches program to meet the needs of their members. But growing churches plan to meet the needs of those outside the church.[2]

This book has emphasized the importance of meeting the needs of youth in order to share with them the Christ, who meets all our needs. Paul writes, "And my God will supply every need of yours according to his riches in glory in Christ Jesus" (Philippians 4:19). Some basic needs are universal to all youth. Some of the needs we have identified are:

- to establish self-identity;
- to build self-esteem;
- to be loved, accepted, and affirmed by significant adults and peers;
- to belong to a network of friends;
- to grow spiritually;
- to develop responsibility and leadership skills;
- to serve others.

A youth program may be meeting those needs significantly for church members but have no desire to meet the needs of the unchurched. There comes a time for each group to decide whether its members will reach out to others or shut them out. Youth ministry then must deliberately research, survey and plan to meet the specific needs of young people in their neighborhood, town or community. By meeting specific needs, a congregation opens the door for building relationships with unchurched youth. Meeting specific needs allows for planning specific activities and events to draw unchurched youth closer to Christ. So, a congregation may determine that needs exist for an after-school, latch-key program. Or, there may be a need for a Christian activity club. Or, junior high young people may need a place to go on Friday evenings.

For example, when we lived in a west Texas town, no place existed for junior high kids to go and have fun on weekends. There was the local skating rink and bowling alley, but, not everyone liked, or could afford, those activities. Some youth had fake ID cards so that they could buy alcohol, or get into the nightclubs in town. We met with some parents and junior high young people to solve this problem. We decided to organize a monthly "basement disco." Some of the young people got together to select records that were good to dance to and had lyrics that did not contradict Christian values. Needless to say, that selection process took time and a lot of screening. Once a month on Friday night, our youth set up a basement disco with music, disc jockey, free refreshments and an adequate number of adult chaperons. Word quickly spread throughout the city. Over 100 young people started coming to the basement disco at our church. Parents regarded it as a safe, clean event for their teenagers. Now, I recognize that some congregations would be opposed to a dance held in their church basements. However, dancing is not the issue here—meeting the needs of youth is. Another church might have set up a Christian coffee house. Another might have planned a Christian athletics night in a gym. Many options are available. The principle is simple: discover a specific youth need in your community and plan to meet it. Meeting that need will open a door for relationship building and evangelism.

Another way to approach this attitude is to ask whether a congregation has a "heart for the lost." In knowing that an overwhelming percentage of people who come to Christ do so as young people, we should make every effort to reach them at that critical stage in life.

The priorities of one fast-growing church impressed me. Growth had made it necessary to plan for a new church building at a different location. The first unit they built was a large gymnasium for both worship and the youth program. That congregation understood the needs of youth. In fact, it had started a city-wide church athletic league for young people. Needless to say, the church witnessed tremendous growth among its teenagers. It had a heart for young people to come to know Christ.

In reflective evaluation, here are some questions to ask about this critical attitude of desiring to meet the needs of young people:

- Are the programs we plan answering questions of both churched and unchurched young people?
- What specific needs are we meeting for unchurched teenagers?
- Do we desire to meet youth needs in our community, or

are we satisfied with meeting just our own young people's needs?

● Are our young people and adults willing to reach out and serve others or do they concentrate on their own needs?

● Do we have a good balance between meeting the needs of churched as well as unchurched young people?

EQUIPPING YOUTH FOR PEER EVANGELISM

After these attitudes have been encouraged in young people and adults, the next step is *equipping* youth in friendship evangelism. Part of that equipping process was described in Chapter 2. All of the exercises and programs in this book enable youth to begin acknowledging and sharing their faith. The Why Exercise found on pages 46-47 focuses on partners witnessing to each other. As young people share how Christ works in their lives, they build experience and confidence. They develop the ability to witness to others. So, when a neighborhood or school friend says, "Let's go hiking on Sunday morning." The Christian young person can reply, "Thanks, but on Sunday I go to church." The friend may ask, "Why?" and the whole process of sharing begins.

Use the Why Exercise to train young people to "reach beyond our own." After both partners share, ask them these questions:

1. How did you feel when your partner witnessed to you? Discuss the importance of empathy and understanding for the non-Christian. After participating in this exercise, some young people may express anger, frustration, confusion, curiosity, amusement and a desire to leave. Talk about all these feelings. Ask if the non-Christian could experience these same feelings and how the Christian could respond in a sensitive way.

2. Discuss the importance of a "relationship" and "timing" in witnessing to others. When should one witness to others? Do we wait for them to bring up the subject of church, God or Jesus? When is it best for us to bring up the subject of Christ? As a leader, feel free to share your experiences after the youth explore the issues.

3. If you were a non-Christian, what feelings and attitudes would you most appreciate from a Christian? What would you least expect from a Christian? Explore how getting angry and

upset with someone who doesn't respond to your witness communicates the wrong message. It is difficult for an angry witness to talk about a loving God. It is difficult for an impatient Christian to witness about a patient God who loves us unconditionally.

4. How did you feel when you were repeatedly asked, "Why?" Discuss the need to be aware of our motivation for witnessing. What do we want from the other person? If the other person isn't receptive, what do we do?

The following scripture is important to remember, "I planted, Apollos watered, but God gave the growth. So neither he who plants nor he who waters is anything, but only God who gives the growth" (1 Corinthians 3:6-7). When someone confesses Christ as Lord, they are guided by the Holy Spirit. Conversion is the work of God himself. We are simply his witnesses. We are not responsible for others' decisions. It is important for the leader to teach the young people that they are part of many witnesses. If a person makes a decision to accept Christ or to follow God's will, the young people are not to take credit for "saving someone." Rather, they can rejoice in that decision and thank God for the many other witnesses that that person may have had. Likewise, if a person doesn't make any decision, the young people can still affirm and love that person knowing that God's Spirit will continue to work in that person's life. God will lead others to witness to that person. Christ is never without his witnesses. So if the teenagers can understand they are not Lone Rangers in evangelism, they can be much more comfortable with sharing the Good News with their peers.

Training and equipping young people is of primary importance to youth ministry. In Chapter 2, we listed many different ways to give invitations to youth group members. These same methods are also effective for group members to reach out to their friends. The more times the members experience invitation in youth settings, the more experienced they will become in offering invitations to their friends.

An effective aspect of evangelism training is when the youth pastor, minister or other Christian laity ask the young people to accompany them as they call on families who visited the church. The teenagers gain confidence as they observe how more experienced adults share the Gospel. This is a widely used training method.

Another systematic training method is through Evangelism Explosion. Youth leaders can read the Evangelism Explosion materials written by Dr. James Kennedy at Coral Ridge Presbyterian Church in Florida.[3] Or, youth leaders can go through that training and then adapt it for their church's training program.

Youth leaders can choose from a variety of training programs. It is not this book's purpose to critique these methodologies. Rather, you are encouraged to survey these materials and choose the method that best fits your theology and youth ministry. Over the years I have had the opportunity to receive training in many of these techniques. As a result, I have become very eclectic in my evangelistic approach to others. Almost every major denomination publishes materials for catechism, pastor's classes and evangelism which can be adapted for your use. Resources for evangelistic training material are listed in the back of this book.

One of the questions I'm often asked is, "What about the parachurch organizations?" Some congregations feel threatened by the evangelistic efforts of groups such as Young Life, Student Venture, Youth for Christ and others. These groups often are active in local schools in extracurricular clubs and events. Problems can arise when zealous leaders or members from these organizations witness to church youth. Part of a church's evangelism training needs to address this issue: What do you do when someone witnesses to you and you are already a Christian? Suggest some of these steps:

1. Listen politely until you know what they are leading up to and then gently inform them that you are a Christian.

2. Don't be embarrassed by your faith. Share what you believe, but don't become argumentative or defensive.

3. If you feel uncomfortable or manipulated, simply excuse yourself and calmly walk away.

4. If you wish, ask what group they are with and request written information about their beliefs, meetings and leadership. Encourage your youth group members to bring you any such information and to ask questions.

5. As a youth leader, be informed and involved. The more you know about your area's parachurch organizations the more you can communicate with their leadership.

The most serious conflict arises when parachurch leaders see themselves in competition with local churches (and vice versa). At times, parachurch organizations may try to build their school programs with church youth. Church young people may find the school club more exciting than their youth group activities and be drawn away. It is the stated purpose of most of the parachurch organizations to cooperate with the church. If a local leader seems competitive, establish communication and work out a solution to the conflict. If conflict persists, communicate with the parachurch national office. Tell them of your concerns and proposed solution. There are so many young people in our society who need Jesus Christ that it blemishes the whole church when different Christian groups compete with each other. The evangelistic harvest is so great and the laborers so few, we would be wise to work together building his kingdom rather than trying to build our own. A resource that gives an overview to what many of these evangelistic organizations believe and teach is **Evangelizing Youth**, edited by Glenn C. Smith.[4]

In south Florida, all the youth ministry professionals had a fellowship, including parachurch workers and local church people. A spirit of cooperation developed out of a mutual concern for the area young people. Our fellowship included times for sharing and training.

It is important to remember that methodology never replaces relationships. Some people learn an effective methodology and go around trying it out on everyone. It's as though they have a baseball bat that's hit a home run and expect that same bat to work as well with every swing. Everyone in the path of their evangelistic bat gets hit. A few home runs may get hit, but one wonders how many are knocked down, hurt and left behind as casualties.

As a new freshman in college, I found myself shunned by upperclassmen. It was a college tradition for upperclassmen to avoid freshmen during the first two weeks. At the end of the first week, I was studying diligently in my dorm room when there was a knock on my door. When I opened the door the student standing there introduced himself as a sophomore in the College of Arts. I was astounded! Here was an upperclassman in the freshman dorm! All taboos were being broken.

Of course, I invited him in out of dumbfounded amazement

and curiosity. After exchanging pleasantries for a few minutes, he began asking me some religious questions. He started, "Do you know that God has a plan for your life?" He went through what I later learned were the "four spiritual laws."[5] I responded positively to all his questions and at the end of his presentation he exclaimed, "So, you're a Christian are you?"

"Yes, I am."

"Then, why didn't you tell me earlier?" he asked.

I stammered something incoherent. He left and I sat there stunned. I never had the chance to tell him that I couldn't get a word in edgewise during his presentation. He had allowed methodology to interfere with relationship. I later became involved in a Bible study fellowship known as InterVarsity Christian Fellowship. I still wonder how many freshmen that sophomore Lone Ranger shot down and turned off to Christ. Methodology, techniques, scripture and sound doctrine are all important. But evangelistic methods exist to facilitate witnessing in the context of a Christlike relationship. Methods never substitute for relationships.

EVANGELISM TRAINING

I strongly suggest that the youth leader study as much evangelistic methodology as possible and attend as many evangelism seminars as time permits. We can never learn enough about how to witness. A process for training your young people could be at a retreat setting. Use the retreat outlined on page 115.

After the retreat, ask the participants to meet for six weeks. Gather each week at a time other than youth meeting to pray, study scripture, and discuss experiences with witnessing. Encourage each young person to share his or her frustrations and joys in building a Christlike relationship with a friend. The mutual support and ideas the participants share are very helpful. Once young people have gone through this six-week period, let them decide if they wish to meet further. If so, make a group covenant to meet as long as they feel the need. If they do not want to meet any longer, offer to talk with them any time they need. Encourage them to call each other once a week to discuss their experiences with witnessing. Encourage the young people to continue to befriend others and invite them to youth ministry activities.

A number of resources are available for these weekly sessions that can both deepen the young people spiritually and enable them to develop their witnessing. **The Workbook of Living Prayer**[6] and **The Workbook of Intercessory Prayer**[7] are excellent guides to follow if the group wants to focus on prayer. In one small group, we followed these workbooks entirely and shared each week the experiences we were having as we sought to witness to our friends. The young people grew spiritually and were encouraged in leading other young people to Christ.

Another weekly strategy is to have the participants keep a spiritual notebook. The youth could use a printed resource, such as this, or develop their own. In one youth group, we had each young person buy a small spiral notebook with divider tabs. The notebook sections included:

1. Daily Bible study. This section lists a daily Bible passage. We started with a study of John, so each week's assignment was a section from this Gospel. A passage was read daily and questions were answered in the notebook:

● The background and history of this passage is _____

_____

● What I learned about Jesus is_____

_____

● What I believe God is saying to me is _____

_____

● One important truth I can share from this passage with a friend is _____

_____

2. A spiritual diary. This section is a place for young people to record the ways God works in daily situations. The record becomes a spiritual journey for the young person.

3. Scripture memory and meditation. Each week youth are given vital passages which they can memorize. These passages are evangelistic truths that describe Christ and how he gave his life for us. Other passages give strength to the young people throughout the week. Examples of passages from each category are:

Witnessing	Encouragement
Isaiah 53:5-6	Psalm 1
Matthew 15:15-16	Isaiah 40:31
John 3:16-18	Matthew 7:7-8
John 10:10	John 14:15-17
John 14:6	John 15:26-27
Romans 5:8	Romans 8:1

This list is just a sampling of verses. One of the most systematic approaches to scripture memory is "Sharing Christ With Others" from NavPress.[8] These packets contain 36 scripture passages. Each youth is given a packet and instructed to work on a different verse each day. Memory packets from NavPress especially helpful in offering encouragement to young people are, "Self-Respect" and "God's Promises." Another excellent resource for meditating on scripture is **The Art of Christian Meditation** by David Ray.[9]

4. Personal witnessing relationships. In this section, the youth record their experiences in building relationships with others. During the weekly sharing times, the youth share what has been happening. Everyone in the group contributes insights into new ways to witness and to build positive relationships. Will Metzger in **Tell the Truth** has a helpful worksheet that youth can use to record their witnessing relationships.[10]

Worksheet/Friendship Evangelism

1. What are characteristics of friendship?

2. Think of one of your friends. What is it about him or her that you appreciate?

3. Think of two non-Christian (a, b) and two Christian (c, d) friends. Answer the questions (last 3 do not apply to Christians) in reference to these people.
How did you meet them?
a)
b)
c)
d)
What are two of their favorite interests?
a)
b)
c)
d)

How long have you known them?
a)
b)
c)
d)
Have you ever done anything of a non-religious nature with them? What?
a)
b)
c)
d)
Have they ever talked with you about a personal problem they are having?
a)
b)
c)
d)
How have you honestly shared yourself and one of your problems with them?
a)
b)
c)
d)
How often during each week do you spend time with them? What do you do when you are together?
a)
b)
c)
d)
How often do you pray for them? Are your Christian friends praying for them?
a)
b)
Have you ever spoken specifically to them about the Lord Jesus Christ?
a)
b)
Identify an obstacle each of them has to becoming a Christian. What could you say or do about this?
a)
b)
4. What will it cost to be a friend (Philippians 2:3-5, 20-21)? What barriers hinder you from giving yourself to others in friendship?

5. What is the relationship between friendship and witness (1 Thessalonians 2:7-12)? What approach to people displays how truly concerned we are to meet their needs (Luke 24:17-19; Proverbs 18:13,15)?

6. What was Jesus' attitude toward people? To what extent was he concerned for his own personal interests and prestige (Matthew 9:36; 11:19; Mark 10:45; John 10:10-11)?

7. What have you learned about yourself as a friend through this exercise?

As the group works together each week, encourage the participants to share honestly, openly and confidentially. They are not to talk about what's being shared beyond the group. At the end of each session, divide into pairs and have a prayer time. Change prayer partners each week. The partners make lists of each other's prayer concerns and pray all week for those concerns. Some of the most special times we shared were when the partners would call each other at a prearranged time each day. For example, my partner and I would call at 7 a.m. We would share briefly in a phone conversation:

- the memory verse we were meditating on that day,

- one prayer request for the day,

- something the Lord had done in our lives the day before.

Having prayer partners drew the entire group closer together. It made daily witnessing less of a struggle when we had someone to share with.

It's important for the adult leader to remember that the purpose of this small group is to support young people in friendship evangelism. This is a learning time in which young people learn how to reach out to their friends for Christ. There will be times of great joy as well as times of frustration and failure. Often the adult will be tempted to step in and try to rescue a struggling teenager. Being supportive is the most important task of the youth leader. Young people need to experience the learning that comes from struggling as well as the joy from leading others to Christ.

I'll never forget a call I got one evening from Dan. "Bruce is ready to become a Christian. Will you come and talk to him?" Gently I refused. I assured Dan that he could do all the sharing that was needed for Bruce to accept Christ. Even though Dan had been through a lot of training in the youth group, he was hesitant. Weeks later Dan came up to me after church and said, "I did it. I shared Christ's love with Bruce. He wants to come forward Sunday at the invitation." I hugged him. The next Sunday, Bruce came forward during the invitation at the end of the worship service. At the same moment, Dan moved from his seat and stood beside Bruce at the altar. Dan's eyes were brimming with tears. His face beamed joy. Friendship evangelism is effective. There are few thrills in life greater for a young person than helping another friend discover Christ's love.

There are times when people get false pride in leading friends to Christ. A Youth for Christ area coordinator, Ron Hutchcraft, makes some important observations.

(Christian witnessing) is *not*:
- changing your friend's religion,
- getting someone to agree with your beliefs,
- reserved for perfect people—God doesn't have any of those to work with,
- an 'I win—you lose' argument with someone,
- doing my Christian duty.

The root problem is that our kids think they have a religion rather than a relationship! It is not a church or a creed or a system we've been sharing—it is a Person.[11]

It is so important for young people to understand that "saying all the right words" is not critical. Evangelism starts with being a friend. Once a friendship has developed, the Christian has to demonstrate a willingness to listen, to care, to be there, and to unconditionally accept the other person. Of course, neither a Christian nor God will approve of all the things the other person may do. A Christian friend recognizes that all persons sin (Romans 3:21-26), and that all need the unmerited love of God in Christ (Ephesians 2:8-9). Still, God loves us unconditionally while rejecting our sinful behavior. Being a Christian friend requires:
- patience;
- listening;
- affirmation;
- refusing to buy in on destructive behavior;
- being compassionate and caring without compromising Christian values;
- being open to the guidance of the Holy Spirit so that at the right times, sharing Christ will happen;
- taking responsibility for witnessing without responsibility for the decisions of the other person;
- having a vital, personal relationship with Christ—we can't give what we don't have;
- being knowledgeable of biblical truths.

Christ's assurance to everyone who shares the Good News is this, ". . . for I will give you a mouth and wisdom, which none

of your adversaries will be able to withstand or contradict"
(Luke 21:15).

Programs for Reaching Our Own and Others

*I*n this section, we will explore specific programs for reaching out to young people, within as well as beyond the local church setting. The key here is to provide fun, positive, comfortable settings where churched and unchurched young people can build relationships.

The first question we need to answer is, "How do we attract the young people to the programs and activities?" Following are some ideas:

Publicize youth group activities through the available resources at your church: newsletters, bulletins, mailboxes, letters, announcements, posters, fliers, word of mouth, etc.

Special youth group events can be publicized free, or for a nominal cost, in the local school newspaper. You also can distribute fliers to the students or post them on bulletin boards. Advertise all youth group events such as musicals, plays, lock-ins, retreats, trips, meetings, special service projects or fund raisers.

When advertising in schools, be certain to use "non-religious" language to describe the event. Include all the specifics so that the young people know exactly what is happening, and where. The key to publicity is to be brief, clear and specific. Liven up the ad with fun, creative art. Following is an example of an ad for a special event:

Sports Spectacular

Saturday, January 29, 11 a.m. · 2 p.m.
Meet at Jefferson High Gymnasium
Wear Comfortable Clothes
Everyone Invited

FREE FOOD, FUN AND GAMES

Sponsored by
First Church of Centerville

Here are some special considerations when advertising at schools:

- get prior approval for ads or posters from school authorities,
- be honest advertising the event as a Christian activity,
- use the ad and posters to create an atmosphere for your church youth to invite others. They can refer to the ad as a lead-in to invitation. For example, "Hey, did you read about the Sports Spectacular in the school newspaper?"

It is very important to be honest and advertise the activity as a church-sponsored event. In south Florida, the public school systems became very sensitive to church-state issues. They adopted a firm stance on separation of church and state. As a result, Christian clubs and events were difficult to schedule on school campuses. One of the Christian parachurch organizations intensified the predicament by advertising events on high school campuses without prior approval. Christian young people handed out fliers about pizza parties, dances and other social events. They also posted them on bulletin boards. The fliers invited everyone to come, but did not say anything about the events being sponsored by a Christian organization. Then, when the teenagers arrived at the social events, they discovered that Christian parachurch organizations were sponsoring the events. Non-Christian kids attending the events were presented the Gospel and a few responded with new, or renewed commitments. Problems arose because the parachurch organizations failed to describe the events as Christian-sponsored. They also neglected to have the fliers approved by the school administration.

One Sunday evening we had an interesting meeting between our high school group and a Jewish youth group. The purpose of the meeting was to encourage discussion between Christian and Jewish young people. When asked what they disliked most about Christians, the Jewish students unanimously agreed that they resented the dishonesty of Christians. Of course, our Christian young people were shocked. "How are we dishonest?" they asked. The Jewish youth referred to being invited to parties and socials held by Christians, but not being told that they were really evangelistic settings. The Jewish young people had no objections to Christians inviting other friends to religious activities, as long as the sponsorship was clearly stated. The principle for evangelism here is simple. Christians should never be deceitful about any activity. We should not be ashamed of who we are or what we are doing (Romans 1:16-17). All of our publicity should be clearly marked in reference to our sponsorship.

No Greater Love

Have you ever tried to explain why Jesus' blood was shed on the cross? Statements such as "Jesus' blood was shed to cleanse us of our sins" are far removed from the understanding of today's teenagers. The New Testament uses the sacrificial system of ancient Israel to build its explanation of Jesus' atoning death. Many young people never think about how animals once shed their blood so that the people of ancient Israel might live. The only time youth "see" shed blood is on television or in a movie.

The program described in this chapter attempts to graphically portray the tremendous sacrifice of Christ in focusing on the concept of blood atonement. "For in him all the fullness of God was pleased to dwell, and through him to reconcile to himself all things, whether on earth or in heaven, making peace by the blood of his cross" (Colossians 1:19-20).

1. Objectives—The young people will:

● learn the meaning of the blood covenant in the Old Testament through role playing,

● visualize the life-giving power of the image of shed blood,
● personalize the fact that Christ's blood was shed for them.

2. Before the Meeting—Plan this program with at least three other adults or youth leaders. Ask them to read carefully 1 Samuel 20. Explain a blood covenant: The ancient practice of cutting a covenant between "blood brothers" or "lifetime friends." It involves an exchange of gifts, an incision in the arm of one and a mixing of the blood with a cup of wine. Both friends drink of the wine cup and vow to provide for, and protect the other as long as both live.[1]

Learn more about this topic by reading the booklet **The Blood Covenant** by E.W. Kenyon or **The Origins of the Christian Doctrine of Sacrifice** by Robert J. Daly.[2] You and the other program coordinators, will also need to read the entire program.

Make arrangements with the Red Cross or a doctor to donate blood. Ask an adult volunteer to give blood during the youth group meeting. It is best that the donor not be involved in another part of the program since a person tends to feel weak and lightheaded after giving blood. Ask one or two other adults to be on hand to give blood in case your first donor is rejected for some medical reason. If you have difficulty scheduling this on a single-donor basis, schedule an evening for the Red Cross bloodmobile to visit your church. Prior to the program, inform the young people about the planned blood donation. Place a comfortable recliner or cot at the front of the room for the donor.

Order the film,"Greater Love."[3] This film is based on the true story of a younger sister's willingness to give her rare type of blood to her brother who was seriously injured in an accident. She naively believes that she will die as she gives blood. This film beautifully portrays the power of blood giving life.

Go to a Christian bookstore and purchase one small pocket cross for each participant.

Ask your pastor to celebrate communion with the participants at the end of the program.

Gather Bibles, newsprint, a marker, and props such as swords, coats, robes or large cloaks, cups or chalices and grape juice.

Collect 24 3×5 cards and divide them into three sets. On each card, write one verse of John 15:9-16, but do not number the verses. Shuffle each set and put a rubber band around it.

3. Giving Blood—When the young people arrive, the volunteer blood donor and the Red Cross employee or doctor should be at the front of the room. Ask the doctor to explain everything about blood donation and about the cleansing, purifying, life-giving qualities of the blood itself. Allow 20 minutes for questions and discussion. Talk about the different ways the young people have seen blood in television shows, movies, accidents, etc. Ask if their thoughts about blood are focused on its life-giving qualities or on its negative, or gory aspects. Inquire if any youth as small children became blood brothers or sisters. If so, what did their covenant or ritual involve?

4. Role Playing—Divide the participants and adult volunteers into three groups. Give each group a Bible and one of these passages: 1 Samuel 20:1-23; 1 Samuel 20:24-34; 1 Samuel 20:35-42. Tell the participants that they have 15 minutes to prepare a role play of their passage. The groups can have different narrators read the passage while others act it out. Or, they can pantomime the scripture and have the audience try to guess what is happening. Have them use props in their presentations.

After 15 minutes, ask each small group to present its role play for the others. Present the role plays in scripture-passage order.

5. My Best Friend—Ask the participants to think of all the qualities of a best friend. For example, loyal, trusting, always there, understands, listens, never gives up on me. List the qualities on newsprint. Once the group has done this, say, "Let's see if Jesus is a best friend." Go back over the list prefacing each quality or phrase with, "Jesus is ..." For example, "Jesus is loyal." "Jesus is trusting." "Jesus is always there."

Ask the young people to think of different scripture passages where these qualities are mentioned. After the list has been reviewed, read the following verse: "There are friends who pretend to be friends, but there is a friend who sticks closer than a brother" (Proverbs 18:24). In ancient Israel the only relationship closer than a relative was a friendship like that of Jonathan and David, who became friends through the blood covenant.

Distribute the three sets of 3×5 cards to the three groups. Give the members five minutes to piece together John 15:9-16. See which group can line the cards up in the correct order first. Afterward, have the leader read the passage to ensure that all the groups have their cards lined up correctly. One-by-one, have each group member complete the sentence, "Jesus is like my best friend or blood brother because . . ."

6. Film—Show the film, "Greater Love." Afterward, give the small groups five minutes to discuss these questions:

● Why was the little girl afraid to give her blood?

● What finally motivated her to give her blood?

● In what way did this film retell the story of Jesus dying for us?

7. Communion—After the discussion, have your pastor explain that the new covenant is Christ's blood shed for all who have faith in him. Celebrate holy communion.

8. Closing Circle and Invitation—Form a circle with the entire group holding hands. Sing a hymn or chorus that the group will know by heart such as "Amazing Grace," "Were You There?" or "Father, I Adore You." Choose one that focuses on the sacrificial love of Christ.

Give the participants each a pocket cross. Ask them to carry it in their purse, wallet or pocket so that each time they reach for money they will see the cross. They will be reminded of the price Jesus paid and his blood, shed for them. As a closing prayer have each person complete the phrase, "Lord Jesus, because you died and shed your blood for me, I will . . ."

JESUS—THE LIGHT AND THE DOOR

One evangelistic task is to communicate that Jesus is the light of life in the midst of all darkness (John 1:1-9) and that he is the only door to salvation (John 10:9). In teaching young people, we talk about darkness, being lost, trying to stumble our way through the darkness of confusion. However, to convey that darkness in a lesson is difficult. This program seeks to simulate a life, lost without the light of Christ and the door of his salvation.

1. Objectives—The young people will:

● experience being lost in darkness,

● experiment with finding their own way out,

● be confused by wrong directions,

● understand the importance of having a friend to lead them out of darkness,

● apply the experience in the simulation to their lives being lived through trust in Christ—the light and the door.

2. Before the Meeting—Well in advance, reserve a large meeting room that is unfamiliar to your group members; for example, a gymnasium, community center or a large fellowship hall in another church. This room will need to have at least four or more exits. You also will need matches, brown or black vinyl strip tape, a blindfold, a large candle (with candle holder if the candle will not stand alone) and small candles for each member of the group.

Before the meeting, prepare the room. Make sure all of the doors are locked, except one. The game works best when the doors can be locked and all the young people can be inside the room to see the volunteers try to find their way out. But, if the doors have crash bars, the young people will have to stand outside and lean up against the doors to keep them shut.

Begin on the center of the floor and tape a path that winds around the room, eventually leading to the unlocked door. On this path, place a large candle which represents Christ and two matches—one at the start of the path and one with the candle (see the diagram below).

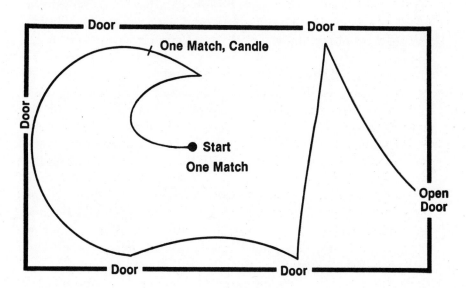

Darken the room by covering any exit signs (check local fire codes before covering exit signs), windows, or skylights. It's important that the room is pitch black.

Go through the route yourself on hands and knees to clock the fastest time possible for a volunteer to find the open door. Since you know the way, add about 30 seconds to make the simulation as accurate as possible.

3. The Rules of the Game—Meet at your church and inform the youth group you are having a special meeting at a different location. Ask for four or five volunteers. Explain that each volunteer will be blindfolded and led, one at a time, into the middle of a completely dark room. The volunteer will be turned around a number of times and then the blindfold will be removed. Each volunteer will be given a matchbook and one match, which he or she can strike at any time. Explain that it's best to strike the match as soon as the leader yells "go!" That will give the person a brief glimpse of the winding path. However, the person is free to use the match whenever he or she chooses. Tell the volunteers that they will be given a certain amount of time to find their way out of the room, by following the path on their hands and knees. (Tell them your clocked time.)

4. The New Site—Load into vehicles and travel to the location. Take the volunteers to an area some distance from the room being used for the simulation. This way the volunteers cannot see or hear what's going on during each person's attempt to get out of the room. Have an adult sponsor wait with the volunteers. Take the rest of the young people to the darkened room. Group them according to the number of locked doors in the room. For example, if the room has five exits, four are locked and one is open. Therefore, four groups will be needed to stand by the locked doors. Remember, if there is no way to lock the doors, the groups will have to stand outside and lean hard against the doors so that the person on the inside will not be able to get out. Tell the group members that when you yell "go!" to the volunteer, they are to start yelling loudly and pounding on their door. They should yell out instructions, trying to convince the volunteer that their door is the open door. For example: "Over here! This door is open! Try this one!" Or they can shout a cheer or rhyme over and over. Give the groups a few minutes to plan their shouting and pounding. Station the groups at all of the locked doors and tell them to be silent until you bring the volunteer in and yell "go."

5. The Game—Blindfold one young person at a time, and take him or her to the center of the dark room. Instruct the person to get on his or her hands and knees and try to follow the taped path that leads to the unlocked door. Tell the volunteer how much time is allotted. Instruct the volunteer that the blindfold will be removed and a matchbook with one match will be placed in one hand. However, the volunteer is to keep his or her eyes shut until you yell "go."

Go through this procedure with each volunteer. After each has completed the simulation, that volunteer may join one of the groups at the doors.

After the first volunteer has gone, ask him or her to help the next person who tries the simulation. The next volunteer has the right to accept or refuse the help of someone who has previously tried the game.

6. Debriefing the Simulation Game—Once all the volunteers have tried the game, gather the group members in the middle of the room and turn on the lights. Discuss these questions:

● How did each volunteer feel before the game? during the game?

● Were the instructions being yelled by the groups confusing to the volunteers?

● Ask the volunteers who found their way out to explain how they did it.

● Ask the volunteers who got lost to explain why they lost their way.

● How important was the first match? the second match? following the taped path?

● Was it easier to follow the path when a person accepted the help of an "experienced" volunteer? Why or why not?

Read each of the following passages and ask how the participants could apply the passage to the game. The scriptures are Matthew 7:13-14; John 1:1-9; 10:9-10. After the group discussion, present some of these thoughts:

The path represented the narrow way of righteousness and obedience in following Christ. He asks us to follow him. If we follow his teachings, we will discover that he is the door out of darkness and into eternal life. If we follow the temptations of the world, represented by the locked doors and the shouting groups, we will be eternally lost. Some of the volunteers may have felt foolish crawling along the path on their hands and knees. Explain that at times when we follow Christ, we may feel or look foolish to others, but the path of obedience is the only way. Although Christ lights our way, there are times when we must follow him with blind obedience. Obeying and trusting Christ isn't always easy. In some ways, the path represents scripture. We obey the scriptures as best we can— seeking the continuing light of Christ through his Spirit and guidance.

7. The Closing—Place a large candle in the middle of the room and light it. Give each youth group member a candle and instruct them to form a circle around the large candle. Turn out all the lights in the room so that the only light is from the center candle.

Sing an appropriate song such as "This Little Light of Mine," or "Pass It On" or "I Am the Light of the World." Read John 8:12 and then have everyone repeat the verse in unison. Give these instructions: "We are all going to quietly hum 'Pass It On' (or any other appropriate chorus you may choose). As we are humming, each of you is invited to go forward when you're ready and light your candle. As you light the candle, say quietly, 'Jesus, you are the light of my life,' or 'Jesus, I'm searching for the light of life,' or 'Jesus, I will be a light for others to come to you.' Then after everyone has lighted his or her candle, we will take our candles outside in silence and leave for home."

JESUS—THE MISSING PIECE IN THE PUZZLE OF LIFE

The French philosopher-theologian, Pascal, remarked in his writings that within every person there is a "God-shaped void." The focus of this program is to emphasize this truth; only Jesus can perfectly fit that void. No life can perfectly come together without him. No puzzle in life is complete without him.

1. Objectives—The young people will:
● learn about "missing pieces" in their lives,
● discuss how God can fill those voids,
● share the fact that Jesus makes us whole.

92

2. Before the Meeting—Buy several 100- to 250-piece jig-saw puzzles. You will need one puzzle for every three or four people. All the puzzles should have the same number of pieces.

Set up enough card tables so that every group will have one on which to work. Place one jigsaw puzzle box on each table and remove one piece. Spread the tables out far enough so that the groups can work without distractions.

You also will need one paper punch and marker per group. Gather some colored yarn—a different color for each small group. Cut the yarn in two-foot lengths so each participant will have one.

3. The Puzzles—As the participants arrive, randomly distribute the sections of yarn. Ask everyone with the same color yarn to gather at a card table. Tell them that when you say "go," they are to work as quickly as possible to spread out the puzzle and try to piece it together. They may not talk. Everything must be done silently. They may not grab pieces from other players. Everyone must help in putting the puzzle together. One person may not do the puzzle for the group. One can devise a system for putting the puzzle together as long as everyone has a part. When a group has finished its puzzle, the members are to signal to you by raising their hands. Then they must sit quietly until the other groups are finished. If a group has a question, one person may come over to you and whisper the question. You will answer, and the person will return to the group and whisper the answer to the others.

Start and have all the groups work on their puzzles.

4. The Missing Piece—When a group finishes and finds that a piece is missing, someone will come over and tell you. Simply reply, "Looks like you're stuck. If you don't find the piece, simply wait quietly until the other groups finish." When everyone finishes, some of the participants may become frustrated. Call all the groups to you. Give the groups the missing pieces to complete their puzzles.

Tell them you will explain in a few moments why a piece was missing. First, discuss the following questions:

● Was it hard working in silence? Why or why not? What happened?

● How did you feel when you discovered a piece was missing?

● Were you competing more against yourselves or the other

93

groups?

5. Sharing Good News—Read John 14:1-7; Romans 3:23-24; Ephesians 2:8; 1 John 5:11-12. Take five minutes to explain the missing puzzle piece in your own words incorporating some of these ideas:

● One man said that all of us have a "God-shaped void" in our lives.

● All of our lives have one or more pieces missing.

● Romans 3:23 tells us that we all fall short of God's perfection.

● None of us can complete the puzzles of our own lives without God's piece—Jesus Christ.

● None of the groups won. Not one group, no matter how fast or skilled, finished before the others.

● We were saved (completed, made whole) by God when he gave us the free gift of Christ.

● Salvation is not us competing with ourselves or others to prove how good we are. Salvation is putting Christ at the center of our lives. He is the missing piece to the puzzle of life.

6. Pray Together—Give out the paper punches and markers to each group. Instruct the groups to return to their puzzles. Each person needs to select a puzzle piece that represents his or her life. Demonstrate this process by holding up a puzzle piece and saying, "This puzzle piece represents my life right now because of this pointed part. There are some rough edges that God needs to deal with." Or, "This piece has a section that needs to connect with another piece. I feel very connected, very close to my family right now."

Start with the oldest person in the group and go around to the right. Have each person share, "The way this puzzle piece represents my life right now is . . ."

Once everyone has shared, instruct the participants to punch a hole in each puzzle piece, put the yarn through it and tie the ends.

7. The Closing—Form pairs or trios and ask the partners to complete this sentence, "One way I need Christ to work on the puzzle of my life is . . ." After the partners have shared, they draw a cross on the backs of the puzzle necklaces and place them around their necks. The partners join hands and pray for each other's need.

When all the partners have finished praying, form a circle.

Take your necklace and comment, "This necklace is to remind you that Christ is the missing piece in the puzzle of your life. Wear the necklace this week. If others ask you what it means, tell them. As you look at it each day, ask Jesus Christ to become the center of your thoughts and actions. Pray with me silently now." At this point, pause after each of the following phrases so that the young people can pray silently. "Lord Jesus, (pause) only you can put together the puzzle of my life (pause). I ask you now (pause) to make me complete and whole (pause). Forgive my sin and brokenness (pause). I give you my life (pause). Amen."

THE BIG GIFT

Each Christmas we give and receive gifts. But one gift surpasses all others—the *gift* of God's son, Jesus. The mystery of God's love for us becomes real at Christmas. God, who is Spirit, becomes Flesh. Here's the challenge: How do we communicate the Incarnation (the Word becoming Flesh) to others?

Incarnation is an abstract idea. The purpose of this meeting is to use the familiar (and concrete) act of gift-giving as an analogy to communicate the Incarnation.

This meeting may be used at any time of the year although Advent is a "natural" setting.

1. Objectives—Participants will:

● share with the group past Christmas experiences and gifts that are meaningful to them,

● explore a Bible passage about the Incarnation,

● discuss the uniqueness of God's gift to us, and

● share their understanding of the Incarnation as a Christmas gift with their families.

2. Before the Meeting—Gather five different-size Christmas-wrapped boxes with one of the following items inside each box: a dollar bill, a clock, a pair of gloves, a dictionary, a piece of sheet music; enough small-jewelry-type boxes for each group member to have one; enough Christmas wrapping paper, ribbon, tape and scissors for each person to wrap his or her small box; an instant-print camera along with enough film and flashbulbs to take a photo of each young person; typed or printed scripture 3×5 cards; **Godspell** and other Christmas tape or album and tape player or turntable; a large wrapped box (empty); pencils; two sizes of candy canes; marker and newsprint.

Read the entire meeting and John 1; 3:16-17; 4:23.

Wrap the five gift boxes containing the dollar, clock, gloves, dictionary and sheet music.

Wrap a large, empty gift box. Make it much nicer than any of the other packages. Wrap the box so that the lid may be removed without having to tear any of the wrapping paper. Place the box out of sight in the meeting room.

Type or print scripture 3×5 cards—each small group of three to six will need one set of cards. Divide John 1:1 into three to six phrases (depending on your group size). For instance: "In the beginning" (first card); "was the Word" (second card); "and the Word was with God" (next card); and so on. Prepare enough sets. Mix up the cards in each set.

3. Greetings—Play Christmas carols as kids arrive. Arrange the chairs in a circle around the five gifts. Take a picture of each person as he or she enters and ask everyone to sit in the circle. Ask the group members to guess what is in each package. Let them handle the presents, but not open them.

4. My Favorite Christmas and Christmas Gift—Complete these sentences yourself: "My favorite Christmas was when I was (age) and what happened was . . ." "The best Christmas gift I ever received was . . ." From your photos of the group members, select a photo at random and hold it up. Ask that person to complete the same two sentences. Continue this until all group members have completed the sentences.

5. Giving Good Gifts—Play "All Good Gifts" from **Godspell**. When the song is over, explain that the greatest gift that God gave us was his son, Jesus.

Divide group members into small groups of three to six and give each group a set of scripture 3×5 cards. Say, "Your group's set of cards contains a verse from the Gospel of John. The first group to unscramble its verse and arrange the cards in correct order wins a special prize. The game ends only when all teams correctly unscramble the verses. Keep working until your team finishes. Ask me (or another adult) to check your work. Go."

Play "All Good Gifts" or carols in the background. Give the first group to finish the larger candy canes, and give the rest the other candy canes.

6. Unique Gifts—Explain: "A gift tells us much about the giver. You shop for that one, special gift that no one else can give. People who have everything are hard to shop for—nothing you can give them seems special, unique or one-of-a-kind. The gifts in the center of this circle represent some special gifts that you might choose for someone you love."

Have the group vote for the gift to be opened first, second, and so on. Open each gift and lead a brief discussion with a question such as: "How does money (or clock or gloves or dictionary or music) represent something unique or special we might give someone we love?"

The discussion might go something like this: "Money represents our ability to buy whatever gift we choose." Or, "A clock represents the time we might spend thinking of just the right gift, or perhaps that we might give a gift of our own time and energy—shoveling snow, for example." Or, "Gloves represent something we might make with our hands like a painting, needlepoint, woodcraft." Or, "The dictionary represents words we might use to write a letter, poem or card to tell a person how special he or she is to us." Or, "The music represents a talent we might use to share a gift we would create for the person we love."

There are no right answers. Don't force discussion. As soon as one item plays out, go to the next.

Then, ask this question: "How do each of these gifts represent a way that God gave of himself?" List the ideas on newsprint. You might need to offer an idea or two to start the discussion. For example:

● money—God created the wealth of the universe,

● clock—God acted in history to show us what he is like,

● gloves—God created the universe to show us his power and glory,

● dictionary—God used language to speak to us through the law and the prophets, and

● music—God spoke through songs—Psalms—to tell us of his majesty and his love for us.

7. The Christmas Gift—Place the specially wrapped, empty box in the center of the circle and say: "This gift represents the most unique, costly gift that God could give to those he loves. The other gifts we talked about weren't enough. This represents his unique gift of love. What do you think is in this box?"

Your group members will guess many items: a cross; a picture of Jesus; a Bible; a Nativity scene. Accept each answer. Then say, "All of you guessed correctly. The unique gift God gave us was himself in the form of a human being, Jesus. I could have selected any of the things you guessed to place in the box, but I chose . . ."

Open the box and show the group that *it's empty!* Pass the box around the circle so everyone can touch it and look inside.

Ask, "How does this empty box represent God's unique gift of himself in Jesus?" This is a tough question. A few in the group may come up with some interesting comments. Remember, the purpose of the meeting is to make an abstract concept, the Incarnation, as concrete as possible.

After the group tries some answers and struggles a bit, suggest this: "The empty box represents the empty tomb. *Christmas isn't Christmas without the Resurrection.* Jesus is here right now in the Spirit. We can't see him, but he's in this room."

Have each young person take a small box and wrap it as a Christmas gift to take home and place under his or her Christmas tree. Then say, "This small gift box should remind you of the gift of Jesus who is with you now."

8. Closing Worship—Play Christmas carols softly in the background. Give each person his or her picture and a pencil. Have each person complete the following sentences on the back of his or her own picture: "One gift I can give to God this Christmas is . . ." "One way I can show love to (a person's name) this Christmas is . . ."

As the group sings "Silent Night," have each person place his or her picture on a table serving as an altar or worship center.

Form a circle, have the group members join hands and repeat after you the following prayer: "God, thank you for your gift of yourself in Jesus. Amen."

Remind the group members to each take their Christmas gift home to place under their Christmas tree and to share its meaning with their family on Christmas day.

"WHO DO YOU SAY THAT I AM?"

This study helps the young people better their understanding of Jesus so they can witness to group members and others.

1. Objectives—The participants will:

● discover the many different titles and names Jesus was given in the Gospel of John,

● research their questions without being judged and embarrassed,

● choose the name for Jesus they identify with the best,

● confess the name they understand Jesus to be.

2. Before the Bible Study—Gather a Bible, 3×5 card and pencil for each young person. Each group of four people will need a large sheet of newsprint, different colored markers and a pad of paper.

Research all the titles given Jesus in John, such as shepherd, vine, way, truth, light, door, living water, life, etc. Write a brief paragraph describing each name by using Bible dictionaries, concordances, commentaries and other reference books. Write each name with its description on separate sheets of paper. Then make several copies of each sheet. Find objects to represent each name; for example, shepherd—lamb's wool; light—candle; door—key; etc. Place the objects on a table. In front of each object, place the corresponding stack of descriptions.

3. Opening Activity—Randomly assign students to groups of four and have each group sit in a circle.

Ask, "Who woke up the earliest this morning?" Then, assign the one who got up the latest the task of group recorder.

4. Bible Search—Give each recorder a pad of paper and pencil; distribute Bibles to the rest of the young people. Have them turn to the Gospel of John. Tell them that John is in the New Testament. Encourage them to use the table of contents if they need it. When everyone has found John, instruct the members in each small group to divide the book up among them. For example, one could take the first seven chapters, another person could take the next seven chapters, and so on.

Give the group members five minutes to find as many names for Jesus in their sections of John as they can. Instruct them to work as fast, but as thoroughly, as possible. When they find a name, they should call it out along with the chapter and verse. The recorder is to make a list of all the names, chapters and verses. Ask if there are any questions and then begin the search.

5. Choosing Names—Call time after five minutes. Distribute a 3×5 card and pencil to each group member. Instruct the recorders to read back slowly the names for Jesus to their group members. On their 3×5 cards, have the students each write all the names, chapters and verses. They should put a star by their favorite name and a question mark by one they'd like to know more about. Tell the recorders to mark their choices on the main list.

Once everyone in the small groups has chosen the two names, ask the students to guess which names are represented with the objects on the table. (Hold up one object at a time.)

Instruct everyone to go to the objects that represent their two name choices. Have them pick up a sheet about each name and then return to their seats. Allow time for the students to read the descriptions. Starting with the recorder, have the group members answer these questions:

●What was your favorite name for Jesus?

● Why was it your favorite? (Assure the youth that it's okay to share the same name that someone else has chosen.)

● Which name for Jesus did you want to know more about?

●What is one interesting thing you learned from your sheet?

● What are other questions you have about the names for Jesus?

Ask the recorder to write the questions down. Have everyone move their chairs to form one large circle. Ask the recorders to read back the questions and then discuss them as a total group. Be open and honest. Share your knowledge with the young people, but also volunteer to do more research before the next session, if needed, to thoroughly answer their questions. There may be questions which have no absolute answers—admit that as well.

6. Banner Making—Distribute newsprint and markers to each group. Tell them that they have 15 minutes to draw a banner that uses one or more of the names of Jesus. Tell the groups they don't have to be great artists.

7. The Closing—Have each group describe its banner. One person can speak for the group or all can contribute something briefly. Place the banners on the floor in the center of the room.

Next, give the students one minute to take their 3×5 cards, go to as many people as possible, and share their favorite names and tell why.

Form a circle around the banners. As a closing prayer, have each person complete the sentence, "The name of Jesus that I love the most is . . ."

Ask the young people to take home their 3×5 cards and look at them during the week when they pray or study the Bible.

PETER'S SPIRITUAL JOURNEY

This program is designed to help teachers or youth workers think of their spiritual journey. The participants will compare their ups and downs with the ups and downs of Peter's spiritual journey. This exercise can be used in a leadership training program to help the leaders tell their story. They then can adapt it to use with their students.

1. Objectives—The participants will:

● learn of Peter's spiritual journey,

● plot the course of their spiritual journey,

● tell about their experiences in the valleys and on the mountaintops.

2. Before the Meeting—For each participant, collect a pencil and make a copy of Peter's Spiritual Journey and My Spiritual Journey.

3. Peter's Spiritual Journey—Distribute a pencil and the following graph which illustrates the major events in Peter's spiritual journey:

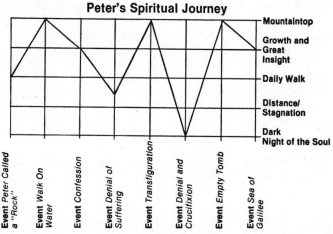

Peter's Spiritual Journey

(A copyrighted resource from **Friends & Faith**. Permisson granted to copy this handout for local church use only.)

73816

On the graph, the high and low points of Peter's spiritual journey have been charted. In a spiritual journey, there are times when God is very close—the mountaintop experiences. These are periods in life when significant spiritual growth and insight occur. At other times, the spiritual journey proceeds on an even keel, a daily walk. Then come the moments when we feel distant from God. We stagnate and seem to be going nowhere. Finally, there are those valleys that Georgia Harkness has termed the "dark night of the soul." Times when depression, loneliness and fear overshadow our lives and relationship with God.

Major experiences of Peter's life have been plotted on the graph to illustrate where he might have been in his spiritual walk. Explore with the leaders where they would have plotted Peter's experiences on the graph.

4. My Spiritual Journey—Now ask the adults to reflect on their own spiritual journeys. What were some of the significant ups and downs in their relationship with Christ? Distribute blank copies of My Spiritual Journey graph and give the participants 10 minutes to plot their own spiritual journeys. Some may chart two or three events while others may chart many more.

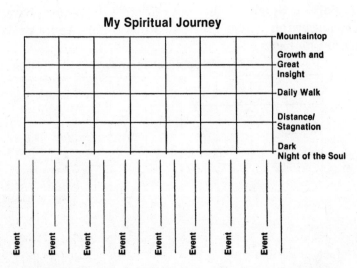

My Spiritual Journey

After 10 minutes, have the adults form in pairs to share their graphs. Invite them to tell the stories about their spiritual journeys if they feel comfortable doing so.

After about five minutes, reflect on what's happened with the youth leaders. Some of the significant points may be:

● Everyone's spiritual journey has its mountaintops and valleys—no person lives forever on a spiritual high. This insight points to the teacher or youth worker's humanity and vulnerability. Point out that it's important for young people to see the teacher or youth worker's struggles, as well as triumphs, in faith. When the kids learn that an adult struggles with prayer, faith and knowing God's will, they will become more open about their spiritual journeys.

● God works in each of our lives in a unique way. We have similarities to one another and to Peter. We also have witnessed God dealing specifically with each of us in our own needs and situations. We become aware of our freedom to draw near to, or away from Christ. Seeing both his forgiveness and love in our lives deepens faith within ourselves and others.

● In sharing our spiritual journeys, we give witness to the risen Christ at work in us and in others. Peter's strong faith and moments of weakness witness to Christ's love, patience and forgiveness.

Share whatever insights or reflections the teachers may have about this exercise and how they might adapt this exercise for use in their classes or youth meetings.

5. The Closing—Gather in a circle and join hands. Close with a silent prayer thanking God for being with us in the ups as well as the downs of our lives.

PARENT—TEENAGER FAITH SHARING

How often do young people and parents sit down together and talk about their faith, their beliefs, their relationship with Christ? My guess is that unless there is a scheduled family devotion time, very little faith-talk happens. Often, the sharing that does happen between young people and parents about Christ is a monologue instead of a dialogue. A young person expresses a doubt, an angry profanity, or resists a belief held strongly by the parent. Then comes the parental lecture about what the young person "should" or "should not" believe, or do. The purpose of this meeting is to open non-threatening sharing between parents and their children about Christ.

1. Objectives—The young people and parents will:

● share what they believe are the "essentials" of Christian faith,

● share their faith stories,

● commit to future faith sharing,

● pray together.

2. Before the Meeting—Send invitations to the young people and their parents. Explain the program so that both young people and parents know what to expect.

Along the side walls of the room, tape eight large sheets of newsprint. Title the sheets: God, Jesus, Holy Spirit, Bible, Church, Christian, Heaven, Hell.

Also tape a large piece of newsprint at the front of the room. Place enough chairs around the room for all who come. Don't arrange them in any particular order as they will be moved around during the meeting. Also have paper, pencils, markers, Bibles and the I Believe handout available for each person.

Play Christian contemporary music in the background as people enter the room.

3. The Opening—As the participants enter the meeting room, give them each a marker. Instruct them to go to the pieces of newsprint and write any words that come to mind to describe each of the headings. Tell them to write clearly.

4. Building Community—Ask the young people to team up with their parents. If some young people come without their parents, assign them to a sponsor. Be sensitive to these kids throughout the session. Ask each team to form a circle with one other family grouping. Ask the small groups to share the following:

● The best thing that happened to me this past week was . . .

● The craziest thing that happened to me last week was . . .

Then have everyone play Symbols from **Building Community in Youth Groups.**[4] Give the participants five minutes to each find an object that represents some aspect of their current relationship with God. They may look for their ideas inside or outside the building. Then have them gather and discuss the items. For example, a person could choose a pencil sharpener and say that God keeps working in his life, sharpening him into a better Christian.

5. Christian Beliefs—After the community-building time, ask the participants to each share one word they wrote on one of the sheets around the room. Why did they choose that word? Allow enough time for everyone to share. Then say, "Every small group is to appoint a scribe (secretary). I will give each group pencils and paper. You have five minutes to make a list of all the beliefs your group feels are essential for being a Christian. Each belief should be written in a short sentence. For example, 'A Christian believes that there is a God.' If it's helpful, you can start each belief with, 'To be a Christian, a person . . .' "

Answer any questions, then start the exercise. After they finish, ask the groups one at a time to have their scribes report their lists. As the leader, write the sentences on the newsprint at the front of the room. After a few groups have reported, many of the statements will be similar. Simply put check marks after repetitive statements.

Once every group has shared, say, "In your small groups, look at this list and discuss sentences that are essential to being called a Christian and sentences that are non-essential. For example, one group may decide that a person must 'believe in God' in order to be a Christian but may not have to 'belong to a church' to be a Christian. Each group can only choose five statements of essential beliefs for a Christian. If there is strong disagreement, then vote whether to keep or eliminate a statement. Majority rules. You have four minutes to make your list."

As a leader, be aware that discussion and sharing are more important than arriving at a "right" answer. The critical importance of this exercise is for family members to hear each other talk about their Christian beliefs.

Once they've finished, ask a representative from each group to share the five choices. Mark each statement on the newsprint. After all the groups have shared, some statements will have received more "votes" than others. Have a brief group discussion on the most agreed-upon statements.

6. I Believe—Distribute pencils and the I Believe handout on the next page.

Give everybody three minutes to complete the sentences. Now have parents sit in a small circle with their own children. Invite each person to share what he or she wrote, beginning

---

I Believe

God is _____

Jesus is _____

The Bible is _____

Heaven is _____

Hell is _____

The Church is _____

The Holy Spirit is _____

(A copyrighted resource from **Friends & Faith**. Permission granted to copy this handout for local church use only.)

---

with the oldest family member and ending with the youngest.

7. Closing—Ask each family member to answer these questions:

● What our family does best to show that we follow Christ is . . .

● One thing we need to do as a family in the future to more fully follow Christ is . . .

During this discussion time, play Christian music softly in the background. Once everyone has finished sharing, ask each person in the family circle to join hands and say a short prayer concerning the other family members. It may be as simple as, "Lord, I thank you for my mother and father," or "Heavenly father, help us grow closer together as a Christian family."

Next, have the family circles stand and put their arms around each other. Lead a chorus of "Love Lifted Me." Sing the chorus a number of times and have each family circle substitute each person's name. For example, "Dad lifted me, Dad lifted me. When nothing else could help, Dad lifted me." Then the next chorus might be "Mom" or "Dan" or "Joan." Or, you can close by having everyone sing together "Father We Adore You" or "Amazing Grace."

Once the song is over, offer a brief closing prayer and ask the family members to hug each other.

WHO MAKES IT?

It's difficult to accept the fact that we don't earn our way into heaven. Being good simply isn't good enough! Not even the pastor makes it to heaven based on merits or goodness. This program focuses on the concept of salvation by grace, not by works.

I first worked with this concept in a junior high group. They had great fun with the role playing and talked about the program for weeks afterward. The program simulates the courtroom trial of a pastor. Many of the young people assumed that if a minister wasn't good enough to make it to heaven, then no one was. I wanted to prove them wrong. Pastor or layperson, rich or poor, religious or irreligious—it makes no difference to God. Everyone falls short of God's standard of righteousness (Romans 2).

In preparation for this program, talk with your minister, associate minister or youth pastor. Choose one of them to play the pastor on trial. Of course, they need to have a good sense of humor as well as be open, honest and not threatened by the youth. Depending on the size of your youth group, each role described in this courtroom simulation can be assumed by one person, or a group. For example, the jury may be a few young people or a large group. The role of God may be filled by three youth—Judge, Son and Spirit—or by one person. The prosecutor and defense lawyer may be individuals or teams. While this simulation is lighthearted and a lot of fun, you'll discover that some important truths about Christ and salvation are learned in the process.

The focus will be to emphasize God's grace through his son, Jesus Christ, "For by grace you have been saved through faith; and this is not your own doing, it is the gift of God—not because of works, lest any man should boast" (Ephesians 2:8-9).

1. Objectives—The participants will:
- realize that no one is perfect,
- see the vulnerability of even the most religious of people—like ministers,
- understand that everyone needs God's grace for salvation,
- understand that trust in Christ brings a person into a saving and eternal relationship with God.

2. Before the Meeting—For witnesses at the trial, recruit other adults or family members who know the defendant well. Otherwise, simply assign some young people who know the defendant fairly well.

Set up chairs and three tables for the judge, prosecution and defense. Set up chairs for the jury.

For each participant, gather pencils and paper. You will also need two envelopes and two 3×5 cards.

● On one envelope print the word "Judge." On a 3×5 card write, "When the jury pronounces a guilty verdict, God the judge sentences the defendant to eternal death. God the Son says, 'The defendant had faith in me. I take the sentence upon myself.' The defendant is pronounced innocent and receives eternal life." Place the 3×5 card in the envelope.

● On another envelope print the word "Jury." On a 3×5 card write, "If anyone on the jury has any check marks in the 'Fail' column then the jury must pronounce the defendant guilty. The reason is simple. God's standards are perfection. If a person breaks one of God's laws, that person is guilty of breaking the whole law. Read Romans 5—8 for biblical background to this concept." Place the 3×5 card in the envelope.

Before the meeting prepare a number of packets with role descriptions. Decide beforehand about how many young people will be at the meeting. Then decide how many copies of each role you will need. For example, if enough young people attend for 12 to be on the jury, then make 12 copies of the jury role-play description. Here are the sheets describing the various roles:

Defendant

(This role should be played by a minister, youth pastor or adult youth worker.)

You will be on trial by God. The purpose of the trial is to determine if you have lived a good enough life to be allowed into heaven. Witnesses will be called to testify to what a wonderful person you are. You will be asked to take the stand in your own defense to answer questions about your past behavior and attitudes.

Be as open and candid as possible to let the youth group members see the real you. Admit your failings and shortcomings as well as your strengths. From time to time, mention your faith and trust in Christ. Allow the youth to see that in spite of your good and bad points, you do love and trust Christ.

Remember, have fun and keep a sense of humor. The young

people may really take this opportunity to grill you. This will be an excellent opportunity for you to build rapport with the youth as well as teach the important biblical concept of salvation. We are saved by God's grace and by faith in Christ.

Jury

It's your responsibility to keep track of the testimony of the witnesses and defendant. On your score sheet, put a check under the column that best describes whether the actions and attitudes of the defendant measure up, or fall short of God's expectations for us. For example, every time a witness or the defendant says something positive about his or her parents, then you would put a check under the Pass column. Every time something negative or wrong has been done by the defendant toward his or her parents, then put a check in the Fail column. Here's the checklist:

God's Standard of Perfection

(These items are from the Ten Commandments and Sermon on the Mount.)

	Pass	Fail
Does not worship idols (including power, success, money)	___	___
Does not use God's name in vain (swearing, profanity)	___	___
Keeps the Sabbath holy (resting, not working)	___	___
Honors and respects parents	___	___
Does not kill (murder, hating others)	___	___
Does not commit adultery (looking at others with lust)	___	___
Does not steal (taking anything that's not yours)	___	___
Does not lie (including white lies)	___	___
Is not envious (wanting something that's not yours)	___	___
Is humble (not proud or conceited)	___	___

Has a pure heart (honest, open, truthful)   ___   ___

Is a peacemaker   ___   ___

Is happy when criticized or persecuted   ___   ___

(A copyrighted resource from **Friends & Faith**. Permission granted to copy this handout for local church use only.)

If you are unclear about what any of the statements mean, ask your leader before the trial starts.

Prosecutor

It is your task to make up questions based on the perfection checklist. By asking these questions, you will attempt to show the defendant as having failed to live up to God's standards. When the leader gives you time, make up a list of questions to ask witnesses and the defendant. Some sample questions are given on our checklist. Use them and make up your own.

God's Standard of Perfection

(These items are from the Ten Commandments and Sermon on the Mount.)

Does not worship idols (including power, success, money)
- Have you ever wanted lots of money?
- Do you ever work for personal success instead of for God's glory?

Does not use God's name in vain (swearing, profanity)
- Have you ever cussed, using God's name either silently or out loud?

Keeps the Sabbath holy (resting, not working)
- Do you ever work on the Sabbath?

Honors and respects parents
- Were you ever rebellious or disrespectful to your parents?
- Do you ever put your parents down when talking with your friends?
- Did you ever disobey your parents when they asked you not to do something?

Does not kill (murder, hating others)
- Have you ever hated anyone?

● Have you ever held grudges for a long time with someone?

Does not commit adultery (looking at others with lust)

● Have you ever read about, or seen in a movie, a nude scene?

● At the beach or swimming pool, have you ever had lustful thoughts?

Does not steal (taking anything that's not yours)

● Have you ever cheated on your income tax, even just a little?

Does not lie (including white lies)

● Have you ever been untruthful?

Is not envious (wanting something that's not yours)

● Have you ever wanted something that someone else had?

Is humble (not proud or conceited)

● Did you ever take credit for something you didn't do?

● Have you ever been disappointed when someone didn't notice something you did well?

Has a pure heart (honest, open, truthful)

● Have your motives always been completely honest and pure?

Is a peacemaker

● Have you ever started a fight or argument?

Is happy when criticized or persecuted

● Do you always rejoice when others criticize you?

Defense Attorney

Your task is to ask questions of the witnesses and defendant that will make the defendant look like a good person. Ask questions that will give the defendant a chance to tell his or her good points. Ask the witnesses to tell all the good things they know about the defendant. Some sample questions are given below. Use them, and make up your own.

God's Standard of Perfection

(These items are from the Ten Commandments and Sermon on the Mount.)

Does not worship idols (including power, success, money)

● Have you obeyed God to the best of your ability?

● Do you trust Jesus as your Lord and Savior?

Does not use God's name in vain (swearing, profanity)

●Don't you usually build people up instead of tear them down?

Keeps the Sabbath holy (resting, not working)

●Isn't your work on the Sabbath for the Lord?

Honors and respects parents

●Were you not better than most kids your age about loving and obeying your parents?

Does not kill (murder, hating others)

●Surely you've never killed anyone?

●When you are angry with someone, don't you ask for God's forgiveness?

Does not commit adultery (looking at others with lust)

●Have you not been a faithful husband/wife?

Does not steal (taking anything that's not yours)

●Surely you are not a thief?

Does not lie (including white lies)

●Would you say that you are an honest person without being cruel or insensitive to people's feelings?

Is not envious (wanting something that's not yours)

●Would you call most of your wants genuine needs?

Is humble (not proud or conceited)

●Don't you think that feeling good about yourself isn't the same as being proud?

Has a pure heart (honest, open, truthful)

●Aren't your motives usually pure, with the other person's best interests in mind?

Is a peacemaker

●If there is a conflict, don't you usually try to find a peaceful solution?

Is happy when criticized or persecuted

●When people criticize you, don't you usually try to learn from them?

Judge

One or three young people can be the judge. If three kids are used, then one is called God—Judge and Creator; the next, God—Son and Savior; the next, God—comforting and convicting Spirit. If only one person is the judge, he or she must play all of the following parts. Otherwise, each one of the three has only one role.

● God—Judge and Creator: During the trial you are to be impartial. Be as fair as possible. Try to always get at the truth. If the prosecution or defense raise objections, always overrule the objection making the witness or defendant answer the questions as best as possible.

● God—Son and Savior: During the trial, side with the defense as much as possible. Be as compassionate toward the defendant as possible while still being fair.

● God—comforting and convicting Spirit: During the trial always side with the prosecution when there is a dispute. Make comforting remarks to the defendant whenever possible. However, when the defendant or witness mentions a failure or sin, always reply, "You should ask forgiveness from God and from those you hurt for that."

If three persons are playing this role, God—Judge and Creator, always has the final say in making decisions in the court.

At the end of the trial, when the judge asks the jury for a verdict, God—Creator and Judge must say and do exactly what is written and contained within the sealed envelope.

3. The Opening—Gather the youth group members and say, "We are here today for the eternal-life trial of (name of the defendant). I need volunteers for the judge, jury, defense and prosecution. The purpose of the trial is to see if the defendant can make it into heaven. If this defendant can't make it, then probably none of us will!"

Assign the young people to the various roles and distribute the packets. Give 10 minutes to the jury, prosecution, judge and defense to read their role sheets. The groups may want to go to the other rooms to work on their lines together. Answer any questions they might have. Give the judge and jury their sealed envelopes. Instruct them not to open the sealed envelopes until you tell them to.

4. The Simulation—When everyone is prepared, begin the role play by having the prosecution call all the witnesses and the defendant to the witness stand one at a time. Each person is then questioned by both the prosecution and defense while the jury marks their forms. The judge makes the appropriate comments.

After every witness and the defendant have been questioned, the jury must leave the room and read the instructions in the sealed envelope. After three or four minutes, the jury returns to the room with the verdict. While the jury is out, the judge also reads the contents of the sealed envelope he or she has received from the leader. The jury selects one person to pronounce the verdict while the defendant stands.

After the jury's verdict is declared, the judge makes the statements as instructed from his or her sealed envelope.

5. Debriefing—One of the most important parts of this simulation game is the discussion. Ask for any questions that the young people have about the game itself. Then, ask these questions:

● Were you surprised that the defendant was pronounced guilty?

● How do you feel about God expecting perfect obedience?

● What is the difference between earning your way to heaven and the Bible's teaching of the gift of God's grace through faith in Christ?

● If we trust Christ and know we have eternal life, should we intentionally sin and fail whenever it's to our advantage or seems like the easier way?

● When we deliberately disobey God as Christians, is forgiveness always available to us?

● What is the difference between Christ paying the penalty of death for our sin and us suffering the consequences of our sin?

● What motivates us as Christians to live up to God's standards?

6. The Closing—After the discussion, close the meeting with a simple group song and prayer. Appropriate songs are "Were You There?," "They Hung Him on a Cross," "Trust and Obey," "Jacob's Ladder," "Thank You, Lord." All of these choruses are found in **Songs** by Yohann Anderson.

Form a circle and invite the youth to pray silently asking Christ to forgive their failures. Invite them to commit their lives in faith and obedience to him. Ask them to silently thank God for sending his Son, Jesus, to be a sacrifice for sin. After the prayer, invite the young people to give the "poor" defendant a hug and thank him or her for risking so much during the trial.

A MODEL FOR PEER EVANGELISM TRAINING

I strongly suggest that the leader study as much about evangelism as time permits. We can never learn enough about how to witness. I found the training provided by the Billy Graham Evangelistic Association very valuable and applicable to evangelism training with young people. Use this weekend retreat to train your youth group members to reach their friends for Christ. Evangelistic training can be done in evening fellowship programs, but a retreat offers a more intensive training opportunity. An excellent guide to help you plan your own retreat is **The Group Retreat Book** by Arlo Reichter.[4] The following retreat programs, described in the above book, would be good training models to use: Let's Be Friends, New Life in Christ and By Our Love.[5]

In planning your retreat, seek to build community and support among the participants. Resources that would help in this process are: **Building Community in Youth Groups**[6] by Denny Rydberg, **Creative Worship in Youth Ministry**[7] by Dennis C. Benson, **The Giving Book**[8] by Paul Thompson and Joani Schultz.

Use the following ideas and time frame for the retreat:

1. Friday Evening—Gather at a camp or retreat center. Begin with community building activities such as games, songs and worship.

One get-acquainted game you can play is Blind Line Up.[9] Have the participants close their eyes while the instructions are given. Tell the group members to line up—without speaking or looking—according to their height. Do not tell them which end of the line is the short or tall end. Have the group members decide when they have completed the task.

Repeat the exercise several times, having the young people line up according to shoe size or month in which they were born. You also can have them divide into groups according to the color of their eyes. Have a "spotter" keep people from running into the walls or getting hurt.

2. Saturday Morning—Morning activities are focused on digging into our own personal faith and knowledge of scripture. Form pairs and do these activities:

● Complete My Spiritual Journey graph on page 102.

● Make copies of a well-known creed of the church such as

the Nicene Creed, the Apostles' Creed or the Westminster Confession. Distribute copies of the creed and yellow, red and black markers. Ask the young people to underline with yellow each part they most like; underline with red each part they don't understand; underline with black the parts they don't like.

Give each pair a large piece of newsprint or butcher paper. Have them make a copy of their sheet so everyone can see it.

Now lead a group discussion first highlighting common beliefs. Then clarify, as best as you can, what the young people understand. Discuss the statements they don't like. Finally, discuss what they think is essential to Christian beliefs. On another piece of newsprint, list these beliefs in order of their importance. Compare that final list with Romans 10:9.

Lead the participants in the Trust Fall on page 45.

3. Saturday Afternoon—Allow the whole afternoon for meditation and time for the young people to be alone. Have the participants focus on essential scripture passages that they need to learn so that they are able to quote or paraphrase when sharing the Gospel with a friend. Examples of passages are: Matthew 16:16; John 3:16; 14:6; Romans 10:9; Hebrews 13:5; 1 John 1:9; Revelation 3:20. Ask the young people to sit very quietly when they meditate and concentrate on each verse for five to 10 minutes. They can break the verse into small segments and recite a segment each time they inhale and exhale. For example, inhale thinking, "I will never desert you." Exhale thinking, "Nor will I ever forsake you." With every breath, the verse pushes the next thought out. Ask the youth to think of a friend with whom they can share about Christ.

Plan free time or games for the rest of the afternoon.

4. Saturday Evening—Gather in pairs and have the youth share which verse is most meaningful to them, and why.

After some singing and worship time, explain the process of friend-to-friend sharing. Use some of the following role plays. Choose one participant to be an "observer." He or she keeps a list of all the religious words the performers use such as saved, born again, God, justified, repent, Lord, Savior, Holy Spirit, faith, cross, grace. These words are familiar to Christians, but obscure to non-believers.

● A friend invites you to attend a football game on Sunday.

116

You respond that you can't go because you're going to church. He asks you why you want to go to church instead of have fun.

● A friend comes to you with a deep problem. You feel Christ could really help her with that problem. One person makes up a problem; the other witnesses about Christ and how he can help.

● A friend says to you, "I know you're a Christian. Can being a Christian really make any difference for me?" What do you say?

In debriefing the role plays, take the list of "religious words" used by the witnesses.

Discuss what these words mean—making sure the young people understand. Ask how they could explain these words to their non-Christian friends. What words or phrases could they substitute to make their witness more clear?

After the role playing and discussion, show them an example of the friend-to-friend process of evangelism. This method would only be appropriate if a friend came to a young person with a question about God. For example, "I don't know if there is a God or not." Or, "What difference does it make if you're a Christian?" Or, "Why should I go to church?"

The young Christian then could ask the friend, "Would you really like to discover God? If so, I have a way for you to do it." The young person says he or she will ask three questions two or three times:

1. What do you want from God?
2. What do you feel about God?
3. What are you doing right now about your relationship with God?

Each time these questions are asked, the friend is to respond with a different answer.

Illustrate the process from your own experience and then model the process with one of the participants. Ask the volunteer to be as honest as possible but not to feel uncomfortable. Should the process get really uncomfortable, promise to stop. Also promise not to say or ask anything that would embarrass the young person. Here is a conversation I had a few years ago.

Bob: Larry, I'm not sure I should be coming to youth group. I don't believe in God.

117

Me: Bob, you sound serious. Would you like to find some answers about God?

Bob: Yes, I'm very confused.

Me: Okay, I have a simple process for us to use. I will ask you three questions: What do you want from God? What do you feel about God? What are you doing right now about your relationship with God? We will go through these questions two or three times, and you will answer the questions differently each time. Would you like to try it?

Bob: I'm not sure how it will work, but I'll try.

Me: Good. Bob, what do you want from God?

Bob: I want to know if he's there.

Me: How do you feel about God?

Bob: Lonely.

Me: What are you doing right now about your relationship with God?

Bob: Talking with you.

Me: What else are you doing?

Bob: Nothing.

Me: What do you want from God?

Bob: I don't know.

Me: You don't know?

Bob: Well, I don't know how to say what I want.

Me: That's fair. What are you feeling about God?

Bob: I hate him.

Me: What are you doing about the hate?

For the first time, Bob breaks down and cries for a long time. I sit quietly and wait.

Me: What do you want from God?

Bob: I want my father to stop punishing me.

Me: Your father or God?

There was a long pause.

Bob: Did I say my father? I meant God.

Me: Bob, God loves you. Does your father?

At this point Bob went into a very heavy discussion of why he hated his father. As it turned out, he had projected that hate onto God, the Father. Once he sorted out his feelings about the two, I shared with him the basic Gospel message. "Bob, God really loves you. He gave his Son to die for you to demonstrate his love for you. He wants a loving relationship with you for eternity. Can you accept his love?" Bob went on to accept Christ and to begin working on the feelings he had about his earthly father.

After you demonstrate this friend-to-friend process with a participant, invite the others to try the process with partners. Ask for any questions after the exercise is completed.

The following survey, What Kind of Witness Am I?, is a helpful tool for self-evaluation and goal setting. Have the young people fill out this survey, then share with their partners the answers to two questions:

● Which one of these things do you do best?

● Which one do you need to start doing?

As a total group look at all the items on the survey and discuss:

● Which are the easiest things for you to do?

● Which are things you never thought of trying that you might?

● What are some things you would never do? Why?

What Kind of Witness Am I?

1—I would never do this.
2—I might do this if I felt God was really pushing me.
3—I have tried this.
4—I do this often.
5—I do this every opportunity I get.

_____I tell people who know me well that I am a Christian.

_____When I meet new people, I find a way to tell them I'm a Christian.

_____I am courteous and seek to serve and help others whenever possible.

_____I avoid being a negative, critical person.

_____I refuse to use profanity or cut others down, even when I'm angry or hurt.

_____I look for ways to wear T-shirts or jewelry that lets others know I'm a Christian.

_____I don't go to places I feel Christ would disapprove of.

_____I am usually joyful.

_____I'm a peacemaker when there is conflict.

_____When I have the chance, I mention Christian values in

119

my writing assignments at school.

_____I give everything I try my best, knowing that God's reputation is at stake by my example.

_____I choose close friends who reflect Christian lifestyles.

_____I seek to be friends with non-Christians without acquiring any of their harmful attitudes or behaviors.

_____I look for people with whom I can share God's love.

_____I befriend new people at school.

_____I'm not afraid of being seen or talking with "misfits."

_____When people seem to be having problems, I try to listen and be supportive.

_____I avoid preaching at people and using a lot of "churchy" language.

_____I know enough scripture to share about Christ without turning others off.

_____I seek to share what Christ has done in my life when others are interested in listening.

_____I pray for my friends, non-Christian as well as Christian.

_____I believe that God loves everyone, regardless of their physical appearance or their actions.

_____I risk sharing about Christ with others, even though I know my thoughts and feelings may be rejected.

_____I try not to judge others by their actions or words.

_____When moral issues are discussed with my friends, or in the classroom, I say what I believe even if it may be ridiculed.

_____I expect God to be actively at work in every relationship I have.

_____Total

0—52—You may be a "closet Christian" hiding your faith. Work on being bolder and living more openly for Christ.

53—105—You are becoming a strong "disciple" or "witness." Keep growing!

106—130—We may nickname you "apostle." You are bold and up front with your witness. Remember, don't let your strong witnessing give you a sense of false pride or a judgmental attitude.

Note: The purpose of this self-inventory is to help you identify your strengths. It also points to areas where you might need to make a stronger commitment. Thank God for the strengths. Seek his power in maturing as a witness. Remember this promise, "I can do all things through Christ who strengthens me" (Philippians 4:13).

Close the evening with a commitment service. Have the participants discuss with their partners, "The one friend I need to share Christ with is . . ." They do not have to say the name of that person, but simply something about him or her. Then the partners share, "The next thing I am going to do to reach out with God's love to that person is . . ." Have the partners pray for one another. Close with a fitting group worship.

MAGNET EVENTS

The youth group meeting may not always be the best medium for inviting unchurched young people. Unchurched youth often balk at going to any kind of meeting in a church building, no matter how safe and welcoming the environment. Special events, also called magnet events, may be the exciting element needed to attract non-churched young people. Magnet events are also fun for the youth group members to plan and anticipate on a regular basis. Following are some ideas for magnet events. Adapt them to fit your own needs, or allow them to stimulate your own ideas.

Awesome Party Nite—One Christian Church (Disciples of Christ) in Spring, Texas sponsors a monthly Awesome Party Nite. David Torbett, the youth minister, describes the magnet event this way. The youth group plans their Awesome Party Nite and publicizes it in the local high schools. Everyone is invited. The fun, songs, games, devotions, costumes and decorations are planned according to a theme. Some of the themes the youth invented are: South of the Border, Old West Night,

World's Largest Birthday Party, A Beach Party in February, Sports Night, Hawaiian Luau.

The unchurched youth who attend Awesome Party Nites discover that Christians can have a great, fun time. Christians aren't always serious, sober types. David coordinates the planning with his adult volunteers and teenage leaders. Some important steps are:

● Everyone who comes is given a registration card. The card is perforated in the center. On one-half is printed a greeting, a schedule of upcoming youth group activities, and an invitation to attend. Printed on the other half of the card are spaces for the participant to fill in his or her name, address, phone and parents' names. The young people fill out this part of the card and give it to the leader. They keep the other part of the card for a reminder of future activities.

● The following week all the unchurched youth are contacted by phone and with a post card. Youth leaders and adult volunteers continue this follow-up procedure for three weeks. Then the youth minister calls or visits them.

● The new youth are placed on the mailing list to receive the newsletter and post card reminders of upcoming youth group activities.

● Parents are asked to sign a permission form for the magnet event. They also receive information about upcoming youth events and about regular parent support group meetings.

David insists that the follow-up is critical. He feels that 40 percent of the newcomers who receive a post card will return; 60 percent who receive a phone call will return; and over 90 percent who are personally visited will return. David and his youth group schedule other quarterly magnet events at facilities such as a bowling alley, gymnasium, racquetball court or skating rink. They implement the same procedures for registration and follow-up for these events. Some important principles David underscores are:

● Have an event on neutral or non-threatening territory.

● Be certain to have registration.

● Give the newcomers Christian information to take home with them.

● Have a devotional time during the event to affirm the spiritual dimension of the program.

● Use part of the time to promote upcoming youth events.

● Make certain that youth leaders and adult volunteers intentionally seek out, and get to know, newcomers during the events.

● Follow through on contacts after the event through the mail, phone and personal visitation.

● During the devotional time, introduce the newcomers to a Team (this is David's version of Intensive Care Units described on page 50).

Sports Team Recognition—A Baptist church in New Mexico developed a unique outreach to the local high school athletic teams. This particular congregation also had a local cable television ministry that enabled them to publicize widely their recognition of local teams. At the end of each sports season (football, basketball, soccer, gymnastics, wrestling, track and field, etc.), the boys' and girls' teams were invited to a special recognition Sunday. The church sent invitations well in advance to the coaches and entire team, inviting them to come worship on a set Sunday.

At that service, the church recognized the entire team and gave them a certificate of appreciation. The youth choir sang and the minister gave an evangelistic sermon that focused specifically on youth and their needs. Each team member was given a small packet containing all kinds of information about the congregation's youth programs and upcoming events. Some young people, who never go to church, found themselves in a warm, friendly, youth-oriented congregation. Many saw friends from school who they didn't know attended that church. The next week, the youth of the congregation made a special effort to fellowship the team members and invite them back to meetings and Sunday school. Through this outreach, a significant number did return and the church experienced phenomenal growth in its youth ministry programs.

Street Dances—One exciting magnet event that our youth in south Florida enjoyed was an evening street dance. The planning process, although simple, was started five to six months in advance. We contacted a local Christian rock group and asked them to play at the street dance. Many of the local groups would play for free because of the publicity and exposure they received. For others, we gave a small honorarium or collected a love offering. We also contacted well-known Christian athletes from local colleges and universities. We came to know many athletes through the Fellowship of Christian Athletes.

Weeks prior to the street dance, we advertised by passing out fliers in the neighborhood surrounding the church and by placing ads in school newspapers. The police granted permission for us to hold the dance in a huge parking lot close to our church. They also provided one police officer to be on the premises during the dance. An early curfew was set and adhered to. Our youth worked hard on an outdoor stage, sets, lighting, refreshments and fliers of upcoming events.

The night of the street dance, the church youth mingled and handed out the fliers. Since the band played contemporary Christian music, the unchurched youth were surprised when it sounded so upbeat. When the band took breaks, different athletes spoke briefly about what Christ meant to them. The kids were thrilled to get the athletes' autographs and to have the opportunity to talk to them.

Hundreds of unchurched youth attended the street dance. Many of them were recognized by our group members and invited back the next Sunday to youth meetings. The street dance became one way unchurched youth could discover that Christians have fun. The street dance became a point of entry for unchurched youth to hear about Christ and to discover exciting youth group activities.

Gorilla Kidnapping—Ask your youth group members to imagine this: You're sitting at home watching a Sunday night movie. You've just taken off your shoes and socks and you're nibbling on a root beer Popsicle. Behind you, you hear a strange grunt. For a minute you think it's your dad moaning about your failure to use Odor-Eaters. Then, all of a sudden, you're grabbed from behind by a huge hairy hand. And, before you know it, you're being carried through the house by a big, black, ugly gorilla. You scream for your dad to save you, but he's collapsed on the couch in gales of laughter.

The big ape runs out the door and dumps you in the back of a van, which is full of kids who are laughing loudly. But as soon as they catch their breath, they greet you with warm words and reassuring pats on the back. You're feeling a little better, but a little more confused as the van pulls away from your house.

This experience is called a Gorilla Kidnap. Its purpose? To

introduce new kids to your group.

Every youth group knows of many kids who would really benefit from the group, but who never come—even after repeated invitations, post cards, and phone calls. Well, the Gorilla Kidnap may be just what you need.[10]

Gorilla Kidnapping is so wild and so fun (for everyone involved) that the new kids forget all the reasons they had for ignoring your group. And, if your regular members show the kidnappees some warmth and Christian love, you stand a good chance of gaining some new members.

1. Before the Meeting—First, your group must be committed to the idea of reaching out for new members. Make a list of all the kids who you'd like to see become involved in the life of your group.

Decide upon a date for your Gorilla Kidnap.

Check with the nearest costume rental company for availability and rental charge for a gorilla costume. The outfit usually includes suit, full pullover mask, hands and feet. If your nearest costume house is quite a distance from you, you can usually arrange to have the costume shipped to you by mail or bus.

The parents of those who are to be kidnapped must be notified in advance. Explain the whole caper to them and get their permission to barge into their houses on Kidnap Night. Also, ask them to keep their kids at home that night. But, it's very important that the parents understand this is to be a surprise— they must not give a clue to their kids about what is to take place.

Next, ask each member in your group to select one kid on the kidnappee list to "adopt." In this way, your members make sure each kidnappee is made to feel welcome. Throughout the Kidnap Night, your "sponsor" members should remain with the kidnappees, showing them around, and introducing them.

Select one of your members or leaders to be the gorilla. Pick someone strong.

You'll also need to line up a van (without seats) or a panel truck. These are best because they add to the flavor of a real kidnapping. But, a bus or cars will work.

2. Kidnap Night—Load all your members into your van, or vans, and take off to your first victim's house. The gorilla should hide near the door. The sponsor member for this kidnappee should ring the doorbell. If the kidnappee answers the door, the sponsor member should smile, say hello and give a subtle signal to the gorilla to attack.

If someone other than the kidnappee answers the door, your sponsor member should find out where the kidnappee is, then lead the gorilla in for the attack.

The gorilla should grunt and roar and really play it up as he grabs the victim and takes him or her to the van.

Don't be surprised if your victim becomes extremely frantic at the sight of the gorilla. Some victims will try to run and some even lock themselves in the bathroom. Some friendly persuasion from the sponsor member may be necessary in that case.

Once in the van, your sponsor member should introduce the kidnappee.

After all of your victims have been picked up, drive to your church or other meeting place for refreshments and a get-acquainted time. Play a couple of mixers that help everyone learn names and faces. Then, be sure to explain to the kidnappees your group's purpose, meeting times and upcoming special activities.

Allow enough time to drive all your victims home again.

3. Follow-Up—A Gorilla Kidnap may be meaningless unless you take the time to carefully follow up.

Sponsor members, during the following week, should each be sure to call or visit their kidnappees—to show concern and to invite them to your next meeting.

You and other adult leaders should send a personal letter to all kidnappees, thanking them for being good sports and inviting them to future group meetings and activities.

The kidnappees should also be asked to keep quiet about their experience, so their friends can be surprised on a future Kidnap Night.

If you don't want to dress up as a gorilla, here's another idea. We had an event we called Snow Balls. The snow-ball effect was created by going, one at a time, to the homes of new youth, picking them up and taking them to our big event. We warned their parents ahead of time and asked for their permission. We decorated cars with streamers, balloons and soap writing. We blew the car horns as the procession traveled through the neighborhood. We surprised the new young people at their homes and took them to the big event.

Seasonal Pageants—Many church youth groups held special magnet pageants at Christmas, Easter and Halloween for unchurched youth. One youth group planned an outdoor, live nativity scene complete with angels, shepherds, wise men, Mary, Joseph, a baby and live animals. The youth built a set and portrayed the scenes of Christmas. Similarly, the Easter scenes of Crucifixion and Resurrection can be displayed. If the church is located on a major highway, the pageant can be set up on church property so that passers-by can view it. Publicize the pageant in local papers and on local television newscasts.

An evangelistic dimension occurs when youth group members invite their friends to work in the pageant with them. Through rehearsals and staging the pageant, their unchurched friends become involved in learning the stories about Jesus and in building relationships with the youth group members. After the seasonal pageant concludes, the church kids can invite their unchurched friends to youth group. The pageant becomes an entry point to learn about Christ and to build relationships.

Many churches and communities are concerned about the negative aspects of Halloween and the dangers of trick or treating. Some churches and parachurch organizations such as Youth for Christ have developed Halloween activities for children in the community. These carnival-style events, often called Scream in the Dark or Spook Houses, take the demonic elements out of Halloween activities and provide scary, but wholesome fun. Church youth invite their friends to help with the setup and staffing of the activities. In the process, unchurched youth see church youth having a great time, in a positive way. These activities are foundations to future involvement of the unchurched.

School Clubs and After-School Activities—In Lubbock, Texas, one of the girls in our youth group developed an exciting Christian activity at school. Parachurch organizations were not allowed at her school. She felt that having a devotional time on the Monday of each week would be a positive thing. So, she received permission to organize a Christian devotional club that met before school each Monday for 30 minutes. A teacher volunteered to help with the group. The club started out small but grew as it was advertised at school. Each week a different minister in town gave a brief devotion and led prayer.

A number of curious students began coming to these devotionals. Some ended up visiting youth groups of those students who were active in churches. Friendship evangelism was working through the initial effort of a Christian student who had the vision and courage to organize this special club.

A Methodist church in Oklahoma City was located just a block away from a junior high school. The youth minister discovered that some of the guys were interested in a weight lifting class. So, he started an after-school weight lifting activity in the church. After school, kids would go to the church for the class. Every class included a short devotion. Church youth started to bring their friends. Later, the church built a gymnasium and developed a full-fledged athletic program for after-school activities. Needs were being met by the church and its youth program. Unchurched kids started coming to youth group activities. The church registered every young person who came to its after-school activities. The youth minister and adult youth workers welcomed newcomers and gave them information describing upcoming youth events. Visitors received a phone call, the youth newsletter, and were visited by adults and youth leaders. The youth program grew dramatically through its after-school outreach.

Youth Centers—One of the most exciting experiences I have had in friendship evangelism came in the development of a youth center and after-school program for neighborhood kids.

Many churches dream of building a youth center—there are two basic options. The first involves building a gymnasium for athletic and recreational activities, as well as for meeting spaces.

First Christian Church in Fort Collins, Colorado, used a unique approach in developing such a facility. The church needed to build a new church facility due to significant growth. The congregation placed ministry to children and youth as a high priority. The first unit completed in the new facility serves as the sanctuary on Sunday morning, the church fellowship hall for dinners and events, and as a gymnasium for youth activities. The basement contains meeting rooms and office space for the youth program.

A Methodist Church in Nashville dedicated an entire floor to youth activities. The young people called it the Life Saving Station. The youth group members decorated the stage area to look like a dock and the snack-supper center to look like a seafood restaurant.

This illustrates the second option of providing a youth area. Young people need a place within the church that they can call their own.

Both approaches—gymnasium or youth center—have evangelistic advantages. A gymnasium may direct its program more toward the unchurched seeking to foster after-school leagues and activities in more the style of a YMCA or Boys Club. Youth can drop in for supervised activities, or become involved in ongoing programs.

A youth center within the church provides kids a place to call home. This becomes their *space* and is a non-threatening environment where they will feel comfortable inviting their friends.

There are certain considerations to weigh before starting a youth center. The congregation must be clear about its purpose and direction. If a youth center is constructed primarily to serve the needs of young people within the church, then inclusion of unchurched young people may cause conflict.

In the planning of our youth center, the church felt that both directions were appropriate—nurturing our own young people and reaching out to unchurched young people. The day came when the youth center was completed. For the first time in years, our kids had their own meeting space and recreational area. Then a new ministry was initiated for an after-school program. As it happened, a bus from the junior high dropped off students in the same block as the youth center. Many of these students had working parents, no place to go, and no supervision until their parents returned from work. We developed a program for these young people. We set up video games, pool, Ping-Pong and a snack bar. We designated rooms for studying and tutoring. We recruited and oriented volunteers to work in the center. We also initiated a special Friday night program with movies, popcorn and outdoor games.

The youth center was open every day after school for five hours. Each afternoon about 50 to 75 young people passed through the center. The majority were unchurched youth. They also started coming to youth groups, Sunday school and worship services. Some of their parents began attending support groups.

The growth came with a price. The church was unprepared for such rapid growth and popularity. Recreational equipment was overtaxed by the increased usage. More volunteers were needed to supervise activities and to organize programs. In some cases, the unchurched young people didn't respect church property or the adult volunteers the way church young people did. Vulgar language and petty vandalism occurred. The church became very concerned when over 100 neighborhood kids began attending the special Friday evening programs. Also, the increased usage of the center meant higher overhead costs for utilities and repairs. Church staff were having to spend additional time coordinating various youth center details. The youth center was costing more in every area than had been projected.

The church youth were also upset. Their center was being used, and at times abused, by "strangers" from the neighborhood. Their cozy youth groups were being "invaded" by outsiders who had different values and behaviors than they did.

The problems were difficult to resolve because of the church's poor planning. Some important questions need to be answered before a church decides on a gymnasium or youth center for evangelistic outreach.

1. Is the purpose of the youth center to reach unchurched young people? churched young people? both?

2. Once the center is opened, is there enough money in the church budget, in an endowment fund, or through income the center generates to pay all the overhead costs?

One church raised, not only the money to build the center, but also enough to cover the center's operating costs. (For example, $100,000 to build, $100,000 to keep the center open.)

3. Who will staff the center when it opens? Paid persons or volunteers?

● If paid, where is the money coming from?

● If volunteers, who will recruit, train and coordinate them?

4. What kinds of ministry programs will be instituted? Who will design, implement, supervise and evaluate the programs?

5. How will the center differ from other community programs run by the recreation department, YMCA, YWCA or

Boys Club? What will be specifically and distinctively Christian and evangelistic about the program?

6. How will the center and its program be publicized?

In the two months prior to our center opening, youth and adults from the church hand delivered fliers and answered questions at neighborhood homes.

7. How will church young people and adults be trained in evangelism?

8. How will unchurched youth be tracked? Is there a registration procedure in place? If a mailing list is developed, what mailings will they receive? a youth newsletter? a list of youth center events? a church newsletter?

9. Will church youth be willing to share facilities and space with unchurched youth?

10. How will the church reach out to the families and parents of unchurched young people? Are there ways to involve unchurched parents in the church or the youth center program?

Once these questions have been answered and after your church has been fully prepared, then a youth center can be an exciting evangelistic possibility. Youth group members trained in friendship evangelism can volunteer in the after-school programs to build relationships with the unchurched kids. Opportunities for invitation abound. Christian young people can invite their new unchurched friends to youth meetings. They can share what Christ is doing in their lives. They can meet some of the deep needs of unchurched youth. Such a ministry demands significant commitment from a congregation in terms of facility, money, time and training. With proper planning and preparation, a church developing a youth center outreach can experience tremendous youth group growth and lead scores of young people to Jesus Christ.

Films, Speakers and Concerts—Some churches go to great expense having one-shot programs with an evangelistic thrust. If careful planning is done, speakers, films and concerts can be utilized for evangelism. These limited events must be seen within the context of a total program of evangelism as described throughout this book. A single evening cannot be used in isolation with young people. Prior to a film, speaker or concert these steps need to be taken:

1. Leaders should be familiar with the message that will be

presented. For example:

● Ask a speaker to provide a detailed content outline of his or her message.

● Preview a film and plan an entire program around it. Films should never be used in isolation. There should be a time to discuss the film's messages and relate it to real life. Just because a film catalog claims that certain films are excellent for evangelizing young people doesn't mean that the films will fit your situation. At the back of this book is a listing of resources. Write for the catalogs and carefully choose films to meet your needs.

● Before going to a Christian concert, familiarize yourself with the music and plan ways to follow up with a special meeting to discuss the outing.

2. Leaders need to publicize the event and invite both churched and unchurched young people.

3. Plans should be made in advance for follow-up, discussion and a time for invitations to follow Christ.

Second Avenue Baptist Church in Rome, Georgia, has developed an interesting evangelistic outreach using contemporary Christian music. Frankie Wiley, the youth minister, organized a Christian rock band called DMZ. DMZ stands for demilitarized zone, a place to come to gain strength to return to the battle of life. Every Thursday evening, the band plays. The church youth invite their friends and pass out fliers publicizing the event at school. After 20 minutes of music, there is a prayer time—sharing prayer requests of the young people. The event concludes with a youth-oriented Bible study and a time of invitation (done in a non-threatening way).

Some key elements for effective outreach present in this program are:

1. All young people register at the event. A list is compiled of addresses and phone numbers.

2. Youth are called and visited.

3. Part of the meeting time provides for invitation.

4. Youth who accept Christ are fellowshiped and assigned to a youth worker. Visitors from other churches are strongly encouraged to regularly attend their home churches. Young people with no church home are invited to become part of the church fellowship.

Over 100 young people have attended this evangelistic outreach and a number have started new relationships with Jesus Christ. DMZ also is planning a concert at a community auditorium. Free tickets will be distributed at the high schools.

Many youth groups have used this form of publicity to invite unchurched youth to Christian events. Free tickets are given out for Christian concerts, films or speaking engagements. The tickets include important information such as time, date, place, event, address and phone number to call for more information.

Drama—A final type of evangelistic outreach that we enjoyed immensely were mime and drama presentations. It was tremendous fun to invite unchurched young people to be involved in the production or to come watch the performances.

We discovered that clown ministry was effective in involving all young people in miming biblical stories. Often our clown ministry team would go to malls and fast food restaurants after visiting nursing homes or hospitals. People would see the clowns and ask what was happening. We simply gave out cards that were printed with smiling faces and the phrase, "God loves you and so do we." An excellent resource for developing a clown ministry in your church is **Clown Ministry** by Floyd Shaffer and Penne Sewall.[11]

There are three settings for effectively using drama to open up questions for evangelism. The first involves using skits and drama or role playing in youth meetings. The young people simply take parts and read through the drama. Or, a team could memorize the lines and act out the drama for a youth program. The drama is followed by a discussion highlighting the questions raised about evangelism and outreach, or about the message of the Gospel itself.

A second setting for skits and drama is Gorilla Theater. Young people choose spontaneous stages for their skits—the mall, a college campus, the sidewalk of a busy street or the high school cafeteria. Very often, these settings have a powerful impact on people who stop and watch the unfolding skit or play. These skits should be brief, usually one or two minutes. Before staging the play, be certain that the youth have permission from the people in charge of that area—school principal, campus administration, mall management, etc. A city permit may even be needed for a sidewalk skit on a downtown street.

Another setting for drama is within the church service. The

plays on the following pages have both been used extensively in worship services to open up a dialogue between youth and adults on issues of outreach, salvation and evangelism. The drama becomes not only a tool for witnessing, but also for experiential learning. As young people act, the message of their dramatic presentations becomes part of their ongoing witness and understanding of the Gospel. At the back of this book is a list of drama sources to give you ideas for this type of outreach.

"Don't Look Now but the World Is Across the Street"

SETTING: A church cabinet meeting consisting of all the committee chairmen. Across the street is a run-down neighborhood in which low-class dwellings are deteriorating. The streets are filled with garbage. As the play develops, it becomes apparent that while the neighborhood is polluted, the real pollution lies in the attitudes of the church members.

Minister: I have called this meeting of all the committee chairmen to discuss the deteriorating neighborhood around the church.

Mrs. Fine: Well, it's about time! It's disgusting just driving to church on Sunday mornings. The stench is so bad from those dirty people who live across the street that I have to roll up the windows in my car every time I drive here.

Minister: Yes, Mrs. Fine, I understand your problem. As you all know, our building mortgage will be paid off this month and we shall have to decide on another project for that money. I should like to suggest ...

Mr. Buildit: Well, as chairman of the property committee, I would like to suggest that we paint our church. Those people across the street take their old, beat-up cars and race them up and down Third Street; that's just one block away. And since that street is unpaved, the dirt is so stirred up that the wind blows it over here onto our lovely white church.

Minister: I realize the need to paint the church, but I was thinking about something else ...

Mr. Buildit (interrupts): No, pastor, I'm not finished. We also need a fence around our church property. The garbage from across the street keeps blowing onto our property and *those* people have the audacity to walk on our grass and litter it with beer cans, wrappers and junk. We've got to keep them away from *our* church.

Mrs. Goodit: We should all be more concerned about those poor lost souls across the street. Now, as chairman of the mission committee, I feel that we should use the money for home missions.

Minister: Go on, Mrs. Goodit, you are going in the direction I had hoped.

Mrs. Goodit: Obviously, we should send the money to the national board of home missions and request that they allocate some of the money for a project to clean up this area and to send some resource people here to lead discussions in our church about the importance of home missions.

Minister: Hmmmm, I had hoped for something a little more direct. Mr. White, you are chairman of the social action committee. Do you have any suggestions?

Mr. White: I certainly do. I used to have a nice home across the street until *those* people started moving in and I had to sell. It sickens me to have to look out of our sanctuary on Sunday mornings and see the trash across the street. I can't worship God seeing the pollution all around us.

Minister *(rather shocked and desperate)*: But, Mr. White, we must try to eliminate the pollution.

Mr. White: Exactly what I had in mind. That world of filth across the street must be eliminated from sight.

Mrs. Goodit: Well, that's part of what home missions are all about. And if we have to go across the street and get involved, we will. I'm in favor of doing all we can with those people. Don't you agree, pastor?

Minister: Yes, I believe we must go . . .

Mrs. Fine *(interrupts)*: You mean we are going to have to dirty ourselves cleaning up that smelly place?

Mr. White: Not at all. My solution is the most inexpensive of all and would still leave us money to paint the church and to build the fence. I move that we use the money to paint all the windows of our church so that when we come here on Sundays, we won't have to look out and see the filth. Only then can we worship God.

Mrs. Fine: I second the motion.

Mr. Buildit: All in favor say "aye."

(All joyously yell "aye" while minister buries his head in his hands.)

Mr. Buildit: Motion carried. Our painted windows will eliminate the dirty world across the street.

(curtain)

Discussion Guide

1. What is our responsibility to people outside of our church? our youth group?

2. In what ways do we as a youth group keep other people away . . . shut them out . . . pretend they don't exist?

3. Against what are we prejudiced? Are there cliques at school or certain kids that we don't want in our youth group?

4. What specific steps can we take to invite those outside our group to come? How can we put up clear windows so that those outside our group can look inside of us and Christ clearly?

"No Excuse"

SETTING: A courtroom with a judge's platform, a chair for witnesses, tables for the defense and prosecution lawyers, chairs for the mother and the clerk. The judge wears a black robe, a traditional symbol of the authority and position of his office.

The judge and Adam had known each other in law school 20 years before. The judge had become a renowned lawyer and later elected a judge. Adam had dropped out of law school and become a derelict. He was involved in a barroom fight and killed a man. He is now on trial for murder.

Clerk: The court will rise for His Honor, Judge McPherson. *(audience and actors all stand—pause).* You may be seated.

Prosecutor *(jumping up immediately and rushing to the bench):* Your Honor, I would like to enter a plea for mistrial.

Judge: Is the defendant accused falsely? Has he been mistreated or denied bond?

Prosecutor: No, Your Honor. The accusation is stated clearly. The defendant is charged with murder. We challenge, Your Honor, your impartiality.

Judge: Would the prosecutor please state why he feels that I am partial?

Prosecutor: It is well known that you and the defendant were roommates in law school. Thus, you will have a bias in this case.

Defense *(vehemently jumping up):* I object, Your Honor. Obviously you knew the defendant many years ago. But your lives separated after only a brief acquaintance and you have not met since. You could not be biased after so many years.

Judge: The defense's objection is sustained. The trial *will* proceed.

Prosecutor: We call to the stand as a hostile witness, the defendant's mother.

(Mother slowly walks over to the witness stand with clerk following.)

Clerk: Do you solemnly swear to tell the truth, the whole truth, and nothing but the truth, so help you God?

Mother: I do.

Clerk: Please state your name and occupation.

Mother: Mrs. Eugene Adams . . . teacher.

Clerk: Be seated.

Prosecutor: Mrs. Adams, are you the defendant's only living relative?

Mother: I am. His father died when he was a small boy.

Prosecutor: I see. Would you describe for the court what kind of relationship you and your son have had through the years?

Mother: I've always tried to be a good mother, to fill the void caused by his father's death. I loved him; I gave him everything he needed—clothes, money, television, car and a college education.

Prosecutor: And how often have you seen him since college?

Mother: Never, until this terrible thing happened. I can't understand it. He was such a good boy. He always went to church. He always obeyed *(breaks down crying)*. He couldn't have done this! He couldn't have killed anyone. He was a good boy, such a good boy *(sobbing)*.

Prosecutor: I have no further questions, Your Honor.

Judge: The defense may cross-examine.

Defense: I have no questions, Your Honor.

Judge *(to Prosecutor)*: You may call your next witness.

Prosecutor: I call the defendant, Mr. John Adams, to the stand.

Clerk: Do you solemnly swear to tell the truth, the whole truth, and nothing but the truth, so help you God?

Adams: I do.

Clerk: Please state your name and occupation.

Adams: John Adams . . . *(pause)* . . . I haven't had a job for a long time.

Clerk: Be seated.

Prosecutor: Did you know Mr. Bill Brothers?

Adams: Yes.

Prosecutor: Could you tell the court how well you knew Mr. Brothers?

Adams: I didn't know him very well.

Prosecutor: That's quite an understatement, Mr. Adams. Did you know him at all?

Adams: No, we simply had a couple of drinks together in a bar one night.

Prosecutor: And was the night you had drinks with Mr. Brothers the very same night that he died?

Adams: Yes! Yes! Yes! I've already signed my confession. I KILLED HIM! We argued and I KILLED HIM!

Prosecutor: And what did you argue about, Mr. Adams?

Adams: Do we have to go through all the sordid details? I killed him. I don't know why.

Prosecutor: But something must have enraged you. What *did* you argue about?

Adams: This is insane . . . must I answer? *(looks at Judge but Judge doesn't return the gaze—looks back at the Prosecutor)* Have you ever argued with a stranger?

Judge *(looking at Adams but Adams stares straight ahead)*: May I remind you, Mr. Adams, that this is a court of law. The district attorney is not on trial, you are. We must establish the facts. You will answer the question Mr. Adams. What did you argue about?

Adams: Religion.

Prosecutor: The prosecution rests its case, Your Honor.

Judge: Does the defense wish to cross-examine?

Defense: Yes, Your Honor. Mr. Adams, did you intend to kill Mr. Brothers?

Adams: Heaven knows I didn't mean to kill him. I wish that this had never happened.

Defense: So you *never* had any thoughts of killing Mr. Brothers? It was just an accident?

Adams: I don't know . . . I just killed him . . . yes, I killed him.

Defense: One more question, Mr. Adams. Did you love Mr. McPherson when you were roommates in law school?

Prosecutor: I **object**, Your Honor. How the defendant felt toward you in college is completely irrelevant to this case.

Defense: But, Your Honor, I merely want to establish what kind of feelings the defendant is *capable* of having.

Judge *(pauses, struggling within himself as he decides)*: Objection overruled. You will answer the question.

Adams *(slowly the gazes of both men meet)*: Yes, I loved him. We shared everything. I still love him. He's the only friend I've ever had.

Defense: The defense rests its case, Your Honor.

Clerk: The defendant will now rise to hear the verdict.

Judge: The court finds you, Mr. John Adams, guilty of first degree murder and sentences you to death.

Mother *(hysterically)*: NO! NO! He was such a good boy, such a good boy.

(Judge slowly dismantles, lays the robe over his platform, and walks over to Adams)

Judge: I take your sentence upon myself.

(curtain)

Discussion Guide

1. Read Genesis 3. How is Adams, the defendant, like Adam and Eve?

2. Do you feel that Adams had control over his own destiny? Explain.

3. Was this crime his fault, the fault of society or both? Explain.

4. Is the prosecutor concerned with a "fair" trial or is he simply seeking another conviction? Explain.

5. When in the play does Adams really confess his guilt?

6. Do you think he was truly sorry? Why or why not?

7. Adams states that he argues about religion in the barroom. What makes religion controversial?

8. Whom do you think the judge represents? Why? What lines prove your point?

9. What feelings did Adams show toward the judge? How

did those feelings affect the verdict? Read Romans 3:23 and Romans 6:23.

Reaching out to unchurched young people can be fun and exciting. Friendship evangelism upsets the stereotyped views of Christian life. Unchurched youth often believe that Christians are dull, sad and manipulative. Friendship evangelism utilizes opportunities to reach unchurched youth with affirmation of Christ, caring, excitement and love. Young people who are unbelievers are confronted by a paradox. The Christ, whom they had written off as irrelevant, comes to them by way of a friend—a young person who lives life to the fullest. Through friends, Christ touches the lives of lost youth who hunger for a lasting relationship with God.

FRIENDSHIP EVANGELISM—AN INVITATION TO COME HOME

Jesus proclaims, "In my Father's house are many rooms; if it were not so, would I have told you that I go to prepare a place for you? (John 14:2). Young people as well as adults long to be home. I talked with some runaways on a Florida beach. Their deepest desire was to be able to find some way to go home. They were lonely, desperate and searching. Some had run away from bad home situations where they had been abused. Yet, surprisingly many had run away from loving homes. For whatever reasons, they believed that running away would bring them peace and happiness. All it brought was pain. Still, pride kept many from picking up the phone and calling home.

Although some young people are on the run from God, much like Jonah in the Old Testament, they still yearn for a lasting relationship with him. They experience a deep hunger for God. Often they can't identify the hunger, or even articulate what is lacking in their lives. As the country song observes, "looking for love in all the wrong places." They need to go home to a network of friends who genuinely care; to adults who build their self-esteem; to a God who has given his all—his Son—to give them a home called heaven; to a best friend—Jesus Christ—and to a family of friends—the church, the youth group.

We have explored the deep needs of youth for relationships with God, Christian adults and other young people.

Are you willing, in the name of Jesus Christ, to reach out to meet their needs?

What is God calling you and your youth group to do right now to reach out to your church youth and to young people in your community?

What feelings have been inspired in you by the Holy Spirit for those lost and running away from God?

What are you doing about reaching youth for Christ right now?

What will you do in the coming weeks to equip your church's

young people and adults to come to faith and share their faith?

Will you instill the desire within all your church members to build positive relationships with youth?

Will you build support for youth ministry and outreach in your church among the leaders and staff?

Will you provide the necessary planning, staffing and funding for facilities and leaders to make youth ministry happen?

Will you start at the preschool level, teaching and nurturing children in the faith?

Will you involve youth in teaching and leading young children to Christ?

Will you recruit, train, and equip teachers and youth workers in friendship evangelism?

Will you encourage your pastor to build relationships with youth so that they can hear and see the Gospel in his or her life?

Will you involve parents in support ministries so that they can more effectively lead their children to Christ?

Will you train youth in friendship evangelism?

Will you implement programs that invite young people to faith and commitment?

Will you explore new and creative activities and programs to attract unchurched youth to the church and to new relationships with Christians that will lead them to Christ?

Will you commit yourself in obedience to be a living witness for Jesus Christ in your daily attitudes, words and actions?

If you, your church or your youth group are willing to take some of these steps, when will you start?

The rewards and excitement that come to you when young people enter into an eternal relationship with God through Jesus Christ cannot be described—they must be experienced. The many young people who have confessed their faith throughout my pastoral career, have made all the work and the struggle worthwhile. No matter where or when the commitment occurred, I was ecstatic. That commitment came because of parents, young people, teachers, youth workers and friends who had paved the way.

For years she listened to sermons, went to Sunday school, youth meetings and church events. For years she heard her parents pray and talk about Jesus. Yet, she kept her faith within. She said all the right things, but never what was in her heart. On Sunday morning, she went to the church preschool to help care for the children. She stayed with them during church time, reading them Bible stories and helping the teacher. I noticed she wasn't in church, and then remembered she was helping in the preschool class that month. Something special happened that morning. At the end of the worship service, she suddenly appeared at the back of the church and walked to the front. She spoke quietly and firmly to the pastor, "I want to accept Jesus as my Lord and Savior today, Dad." The congregation, her mother, and I wept and rejoiced. All of her church experiences had played a part in her decision and faith; all the programs, all the retreats, all the long hours in prayer had paid off.

A youth group needs an environment where they can come home to God. A community where they can find affirmation, joy, stimulation, challenge and the risen Christ. Where do they find such a place? Perhaps this story can say it best:

I was sitting in my study late in the afternoon when the phone rang. My first inclination was not to answer it. It was after 5 p.m. and no one would expect me to be in the office. But, after many rings, I gave in. When I answered, the man on the other end of the line asked me if I was the pastor. "I am."

He sighed, "I'm a pastor here in Iowa and got your name from the denominational directory. Could you help me?" Not knowing what he needed, I naively volunteered to help. "My son ran away from home two days ago. My wife and I have been worried sick. The police have been out looking everywhere for him. We feared he had been abducted or even killed. But he called a few minutes ago from your town. He ran away from home to go to my brother's house in Austin. He's at a pay phone at the north end of Waco. Would you go get him and put him on a bus back to Iowa for us?"

The desperate pastor continued to tell the son's story. He related that a few months ago he and his family had moved from Austin to Iowa. For years, he had served a church in Austin. Most of his family lived there as well. His son had grown up in Austin and was a junior in high school when they had moved to Iowa. The son enjoyed school and had become very close to his aunt and uncle in Austin. The son hated the move. Iowa was much different than Austin. He had problems adjusting to new kids at school and to the different culture. He acted on his displeasure, and became a discipline problem at school. Finally, he was suspended. He had been working at a fast-food restaurant. So, he took his paycheck, packed some clothes when Mom and Dad were at work, and hitchhiked to Austin. Two days later, in Waco, he ran out of money. In desperation, he finally called home.

I listened to the father's story. I dreaded what he asked me to do. What if David (not his real name) didn't want to go home? What if he refused to talk with me? The father gave me the location of the pay phone. As I hung up the phone and drove to meet David, I wondered what I was getting into. I found the pay phone outside of a convenience store. Inside I found David spending his last quarter on a video game.

"Are you David?" I asked.

"Yeah, who are you?"

"I'm Larry, a minister here in town who your father called," I explained.

"So?" he asked.

"So, your father and mother want me to take you to the bus depot and get you a ticket back home."

"Home is Austin," he sullenly answered and went back to his video game.

"What now?" I thought to myself. "Are you hungry?" Any junior in high school would be hungry most any time.

"Yeah."

"Would you like me to take you to the bus station? There's a cafe there and we could talk while you eat something."

"Okay," he responded. "But there's no way I'm going to Iowa."

All the way to the bus station, I sought to build a relationship with David. Slowly, he warmed up. He talked about how he hated Iowa. He shared how angry he was with his dad for moving away from Austin. He told me how much he wanted to go home–to Austin–and live with his aunt and uncle. I frantically wondered how I might talk him into going back to his parents.

As we entered the bus station, the loudspeaker was blaring, "Bus now loading for Temple, Austin, San Antonio and points south. All aboard please." I panicked. David grabbed my arm. "Buy me a ticket for that bus, please." It was one of those situations where there was no time to think, to weigh the pros and cons. A decision had to be made right away.

"Listen," I said. "I'll get you a ticket to Austin but wait and eat something first. There are buses every hour between here and Austin. You can take the next one if you decide to."

"Okay," he replied. We bought the ticket. He put it in his backpack for safekeeping.

We walked next door to the cafe. It was closed! Nothing seemed to be going right. "Let's go to McDonald's," I suggested. "It's just around the corner."

David paused. He was beat, exhausted from traveling day and night on the road. "Can't we just sit here?" he asked.

"Sure," I reasoned. "I'll just go around the corner and get you something quickly and bring it back." That was fine with David. Down the block, I went to McDonald's. The lobby was crowded with the football crowd on their way to a local high school game, so I went outside to the drive-up window to order. I hurried back to the bus station with the food. As I rounded the corner, a bus was pulling out. All of a sudden, it hit me, "David could be taking off!"

Of course, that's exactly what he was doing. Inside the station there was no trace of David. "He must be on the bus," I thought. Jumping into my car, I started chasing the bus down the main street in Waco. Finally, there was a red light. The bus stopped. I pulled up beside it. I grabbed the McDonald's bag and jumped out of my car. I started pounding on the bus door. The bus driver gave me a strange look. David saw me and asked the driver to open the door. Not trusting me, the bus driver only opened the door slightly. David reached for the bag of food. He shouted, "Thanks!" The door shut. And off the bus went into the darkness.

So that was it. David was on his way to Austin. I headed back home. I prayed, "Lord, let David get to Austin and call his parents before they call me." The Lord works in mysterious ways.

As I set foot inside the front door at home, the phone was ringing. My wife answered. "It's for you. Some minister in Iowa." As I picked up the receiver, I had that guilty feeling of being caught red-handed. I decided that if I didn't volunteer too much information maybe I would get off the hook.

"Did you find David?" he asked.

"Yes."

"Was he okay?"

"He was fine," I replied.

"Did you put him on a bus home?"

"Yes." I simply didn't define where home was.

"When will he be here?" David's father anxiously asked.

This was the moment of truth. "I don't know." Maybe the long distance line would go dead, right now!

"What do you mean?"

There was no putting off David's father any longer. "David is on the bus to Austin. He wants to live with his uncle. Sorry, but that's the best I could do."

David's father said some angry things and hung up on me. It wasn't until two weeks later that I found out what happened when David arrived in Austin. I received a letter from David's father. He told me the rest of the story.

After David's father had hung up on me, he and David's mother had a long talk. They came to the conclusion that they weren't handling the situation very well. So, David's dad got on the phone to his brother in Austin. He told his brother, "David is traveling by bus to Austin. Would you go down to the station right away so you can be there when he arrives? And, when David gets off the bus would you go and hug him for me? Tell him for us, 'Your mom and dad love you very much. We'll work all this out. David, welcome home.' "

Young people need to come home to God. How wonderful it is when the church and its youth ministry extends its arms, offering a hug of love and saying, "Your Father loves you, welcome home!"

NOTES FOR CHAPTER 1

[1]David Elkind, **All Grown Up and No Place to Go** (Reading, MA: Addison-Wesley, 1984), pp. 70-71.

[2]Search Institute, **Young Adolescents and Their Parents** (Minneapolis: Search Institute, 1984), p. 97.

[3]Ibid., p. 55.

[4]Merton P. Strommen, **Five Cries of Youth** (San Francisco: Harper and Row, 1979), p. 29.

[5]George Gallup, Jr. and David Poling, **The Search for America's Faith** (Nashville: Abingdon, 1980), pp. 30-31.

[6]Ibid., p. 39.

[7]Howard Clinebell, **Growth Counseling** (Nashville: Abingdon, 1979), p. 27.

[8]Charles T. Robinson, "Somebody Comes Enough," **Alive Now** (Nov./Dec. 1980):21.

[9]Martin Marty, **Friendship** (Allen, TX: Argus, 1980), p. 117.

[10]Herb Miller, **National Evangelism Team Leader's Guide** (Lubbock, TX: Net Press, 1979), p. 2.

[11]"Can We Help You?" **Church Management: The Clergy Journal** (February 1975).

[12]Herb Miller, **Fishing on the Asphalt** (St. Louis: Bethany Press, 1983), p. 77.

[13]John H. Westerhoff III, **Bringing Up Children in the Christian Faith** (Minneapolis: Winston Press, 1980), p. 26.

[14]Ibid., p. 26.

[15]Gallup and Poling, **The Search for America's Faith**, p. 18.

[16]Ibid., p. 20.

[17]Search Institute, **Young Adolescents and Their Parents**, pp. 97, 132.

NOTES FOR CHAPTER 2

[1]James Dobson, **Focus on the Family** available from Word, Inc., Box 1790, Waco, TX 76796.

[2]**Group's JR. HIGH MINISTRY**, Box 481, Loveland, CO 80539.

[3]James W. Fowler, **Stages of Faith** (San Francisco: Harper and Row, 1981), p. 159.

[4]William Clemmons, "A New Art: Relational Thinking," **Faith at Work** (September 1974).

[4]J. David Stone, **Catching the Rainbow: A Total-Concept Youth Ministry** (Nashville: Abingdon, 1981), Chapter 1.

[6]Lyman Coleman, **Encyclopedia of Serendipity** (Littleton, CO: Serendipity House, 1979).

[7]**The Children's Living Bible** (Wheaton, IL: Tyndale House, 1970).

[8]Search Institute, **Young Adolescents and Their Parents** (Minneapolis: Search Institute, 1984), p. 40.

[9]Glenn C. Smith, ed., **Evangelizing Youth** (Wheaton, IL: Tyndale House, 1985), p. 122.

[10]**Youth Ministry Resources, Volume III** (Washington, D.C.: U.S. Catholic Conference, Department of Education, 1979), Section: Theory of Youth Ministry. Used with permission.

[11]Kennon L. Callahan, **Twelve Keys to an Effective Church** (San Francisco: Harper and Row, 1983), p. 12.

NOTES FOR CHAPTER 3

[1]Search Institute, **Young Adolescents and Their Parents** (Minneapolis: Search Institute, 1984), p. 97.

[2]Robert H. Schuller, **Your Church Has Real Possibilities** (Glendale, CA: Gospel Light Publications, 1974), pp. 159ff.

[3]"Evangelism Explosion" materials available from Tyndale House, 336 Gunderson Dr., Wheaton, IL 60189.

[4]Glenn C. Smith, ed., **Evangelizing Youth** (Wheaton, IL: Tyndale House, 1985).

[5]"Evangelism Explosion" materials available from Tyndale House.

[6]Maxie D. Dunnam, **The Workbook of Living Prayer** (Nashville: The Upper Room, 1975).

[7]Maxie D. Dunnam, **The Workbook of Intercessory Prayer** (Nashville: The Upper Room, 1979).

[8]"Sharing Christ With Others" packet available from Nav-Press, Box 6000, Colorado Springs, CO 80934.

[9]**The Art of Christian Meditation**, by David Ray, is available

from Pocket Books, 1230 Avenue of the Americas, New York, NY 10020.

[10]Taken from pp. 165-166 of **Tell the Truth** by Will Metzger. ©1981 by InterVarsity Christian Fellowship of the USA and used by permission of InterVarsity Press, Downers Grove, IL 60515.

[11]Smith, **Evangelizing Youth**, p. 123.

NOTES FOR CHAPTER 4

[1]E.W. Kenyon, **The Blood Covenant** (Lynnwood, WA: Kenyon Gospel Publishing Society, 1969), pp. 5-13.

[2]Robert J. Daly, **The Origin of the Christian Doctrine of Sacrifice** (Philadelphia: Fortress Press, 1978), pp. 1-40.

[3]**Greater Love** available from Mass Media Ministries, 2116 North Charles St., Baltimore, MD 21218, (301) 727-3270, and other distributors.

[4]Denny Rydberg, **Building Community in Youth Groups** (Loveland, CO: Group Books, 1985), pp. 70-71.

[5]Arlo Reichter, **The Group Retreat Book** (Loveland, CO: Group Books, 1983), pp. 152, 190, 212.

[6]Rydberg, **Building Community in Youth Groups.**

[7]Dennis C. Benson, **Creative Worship in Youth Ministry** (Loveland, CO: Group Books, 1985).

[8]Paul Thompson and Joani Schultz, **The Giving Book** (Atlanta: John Knox Press, 1985).

[9]Rydberg, **Building Community in Youth Groups**, p. 34.

[10]Lee Sparks, ed., **The Youth Group How-To Book** (Loveland, CO: Group Books, 1981), pp. 26-27.

[11]Floyd Shaffer and Penne Sewall, **Clown Ministry** (Loveland, CO: Group Books, 1984).

Resources

Aldrich, Joseph C. **Lifestyle Evangelism**. Portland: Multnomah Press, 1981. The most helpful sections in this text for youth evangelism are Chapters 6, 7 and 8. Aldrich encourages us to develop a life that embodies Christ in the world. Particularly helpful are his questions on determining a person's readiness to hear the Gospel and how to ask what he calls the "pilgrimage question." This book is particularly helpful in equipping adults for friendship evangelism with youth.

Anderson, Yohann. **Songs**. San Anselmo, CA: Songs and Creations, 1972. This book includes over 580 songs for camps, retreats, church or youth meetings. Guitar chords accompany the words; however, a **Tune Book** is also available which has melody lines.

Armstrong, Richard Stoll. **Service Evangelism**. Philadelphia: Westminster Press, 1979. This book explores the program titled P.R.O.O.F. (Probing Responsibly Our Own Faith). The author gives helpful examples for role playing and communication skills in evangelism. Specific exercises that help train youth or adults for evangelism are found in Chapters 5 and 6. A beneficial model for conducting an evangelism training seminar is given in step-by-step form.

Benson, Dennis C. **Creative Worship in Youth Ministry**. Loveland, CO: Group Books, 1985. This book is most helpful for developing meaningful worship. Some of the models with an evangelistic theme are God's Mosaic, Sin and Jesus, Identity, Stronger Faith, The New Driver and The Family Chalice.

Callahan, Kennon L. **Twelve Keys to an Effective Church**. San Francisco: Harper and Row, 1983. While this book is not specifically directed toward evangelism, helpful insights abound for the church leader, pastor, youth worker and church staff for understanding the dynamics of the total church. Evangelism, as the task of the entire church, is put into perspective by Callahan's thoughtful treatment. Especially relevant to this study in friendship evangelism with youth are the first six chapters. Callahan emphasizes, "People win people to Christ; programs do not. People discover people in significant relational groups, not in a merry-go-round of programs and activities."

Coleman, Lyman. **Encyclopedia of Serendipity**. Littleton, CO: Serendipity House, 1976. Although some of the exercises are dated, this compendium of small group exercises is still a valuable resource for community building with youth. Especially helpful for friendship evangelism training are the exercises Scripture Happenings and Scripture Heavies.

Dunnam, Maxie. **The Workbook of Living Prayer** and **The Workbook of Intercessory Prayer**. Nashville: The Upper Room, 1975. Both of these guides provide concrete studies to be used by youth following friendship evangelism training. These guides are best used in a small group. Both have excellent leader's notes for conducting small group sessions.

Fowler, James W. **Stages of Faith**. San Francisco: Harper and Row, 1981. This text is critical for learning how young people come to understand faith. It should be required reading for all teachers and youth workers who are responsible for developing relationships with youth and training other adults. Particularly helpful are Chapters 7 and 8. The book will also aid adults in understanding their own faith journeys.

Larson, Bruce. **The Relational Revolution**. Waco, TX: Word, 1976. Bruce Larson documents the emerging focus on relationships in society, the church and theology. Especially helpful for youth ministry is the chapter Identity—the Ultimate Search.

Merrill, Dean and Shelley, Marshall, ed. **Fresh Ideas for Preaching**. Waco, TX: Word, 1984. Practical, concrete evangelism ideas are provided in the chapter Reaching Out. Many of these may be adapted for working with youth.

Marty, Martin E. **Friendship**. Allen, TX: Argus, 1980. Older youth and adults could use this book for devotional reading and for developing an understanding of the importance of friendship. This book might be used as a Sunday school text if a teacher were willing to develop a study guide.

Metzger, Will. **Tell the Truth**. Downers Grove, IL: InterVarsity Press, 1981. Metzger's emphasis on the holiness and sovereignty of God is most helpful. The tables provided on pages 32, 46 and 165 are useful in training adults and youth in evangelism.

McGavran, Donald and Hunter, George C. **Church Growth: Strategies That Work**. Nashville: Abingdon, 1980. This standard text conceptualizes evangelism from a total congregational perspective. Most helpful are the concepts on how to mobilize an outreach-conscious congregation.

Miller, Herb. **Evangelism's Open Secrets**. St. Louis: Bethany Press, 1977. Practical evangelism concepts for training youth and adults abound in this book. Especially relevant for friendship evangelism is the chapter Overcoming Theological Hangups.

Miller, Herb. **Fishing on the Asphalt**. St. Louis: Bethany Press, 1983. Again, Miller's practical insights into congregations are valuable for training. His comments about the relationship between youth work and evangelism are worth noting.

Miller, Keith. **A Taste of New Wine**. Waco, TX: Word, 1965. This classic book on Christian relationships, renewal and lifestyles focuses on living a transparent Christian life.

Reichter, Arlo. **The Group Retreat Book**. Loveland, CO: Group Books, 1983. The retreats outlined in this book are excellent examples to follow when planning your own retreats. Retreats with an evangelistic thrust are New Life in Christ and Walkin' in the Light.

Rydberg, Denny. **Building Community in Youth Groups**. Loveland, CO: Group Books, 1985. Denny's book provides excellent ideas for building community in your group. A practical five-step plan offers activities to help your group grow, focusing attention on trust, caring and God's love.

Smith, Glenn C., ed. **Evangelizing Youth**. Wheaton, IL: Tyndale House, 1985. An excellent resource for documenting what various denominations, organizations and parachurch groups are doing in youth evangelism. Most descriptions also detail the methodology and philosophy of these groups.

Shaffer, Floyd and Sewall, Penne. **Clown Ministry**. Loveland, CO: Group Books, 1984. Clowning is one of the most helpful experiences in freeing young people of their inhibitions about sharing faith with others. Youth seem more open and relaxed using the clown to share Christ's love. This book prepares its readers for clown ministry.

Stone, J. David. **Catching the Rainbow: A Total-Concept Youth Ministry**. Nashville: Abingdon, 1981. This anthology of youth ministry articles provides an excellent background for developing a model of friendship youth ministry. Especially helpful are the chapters Catching the Rainbow, Compassionate Youth Ministry, Youth to Youth and Body Builders.

Thompson, Paul and Schultz, Joani. **The Giving Book**. Atlanta: John Knox Press, 1985. Many individual worship moments and complete worship settings are detailed by Paul and Joani. Community building and evangelistic worship concepts are found in No Strings Attached, Forgiving—Creating a World Without Walls and Giving God Our Best.

Westerhoff, John H. III. **Bringing Up Children in the Christian Faith**. Minneapolis: Winston Press, 1980. This is an important book for parents of preschool and elementary age children. It will help parents identify ways they can work with their children in faith formation.

SPIRITUAL GROWTH IN YOUTH MINISTRY, BY J. DAVID STONE. Offers help for youth workers to grow in their relationship with God. Also offers incredible opportunities for spiritual growth in youth groups. Hardbound. $12.95.

CREATIVE WORSHIP IN YOUTH MINISTRY, BY DENNIS C. BENSON. An ideas-packed resource for youth worship in various settings—Youth Sundays, youth group meetings, retreats and camps, many more. $11.95.

THE YOUTH GROUP MEETING GUIDE, BY RICHARD W. BIMLER. This resource provides years of inspiration, ideas and programs for the most common youth group activity—the meeting. $11.95.

THE BEST OF TRY THIS ONE (Volume 1). A fun collection of games, crowdbreakers and programs from GROUP Magazine's "Try This One" section. $5.95.

MORE . . . TRY THIS ONE (Volume 2). A bonanza of youth group ideas—crowdbreakers, stunts, games, discussions and fund raisers. $5.95.

TRY THIS ONE . . . TOO (Volume 3). Scores of creative youth ministry ideas. $5.95.

TRY THIS ONE . . . STRIKES AGAIN (Volume 4). A gold mine of original, simple and fun youth group activities. $5.95.

FRIEND TO FRIEND, BY J. DAVID STONE & LARRY KEEFAUVER. Provides a simple yet powerful method for helping a friend sort through thoughts, feelings and behaviors of life problems. $4.95.

PEW PEEVES. A humorous look at all those little things that drive you crazy in church. $3.95.

Available at Christian bookstores or directly from the publisher: Group Books, Box 481, Loveland, CO 80539. Enclose $2 for postage and handling with each order from the publisher.